THE SCIENCE OF
POSITIVITY

STOP NEGATIVE
THOUGHT PATTERNS
— BY —
CHANGING YOUR
BRAIN CHEMISTRY

THE SCIENCE OF
POSITIVITY

LORETTA GRAZIANO BREUNING, PHD
AUTHOR OF *HABITS OF A HAPPY BRAIN*

Adams Media
New York London Toronto Sydney New Delhi

Adams Media
An Imprint of Simon & Schuster, Inc.
100 Technology Center Drive
Stoughton, MA 02072
Copyright © 2017 by Loretta Graziano Breuning.

For information about special discounts for bulk purchases, please contact Simon & Schuster Special Sales at 1-866-506-1949 or business@simonandschuster.com.

The Simon & Schuster Speakers Bureau can bring authors to your live event. For more information or to book an event contact the Simon & Schuster Speakers Bureau at 1-866-248-3049 or visit our website at www.simonspeakers.com.

Manufactured in the United States of America

8 2022

Library of Congress Cataloging-in-Publication Data has been applied for.

ISBN 978-1-4405-9965-1
ISBN 978-1-4405-9966-8 (ebook)

DEDICATION

For my children, Lauren and Kyle, who helped me learn about the brain from the bottom up.

TABLE OF CONTENTS

INTRODUCTION

Anyone can feel positive. Anyone can enjoy the happy brain chemicals that positivity unleashes.

That may seem foolish because the bad in the world is so obvious. Negativity may seem like an intelligent response to the world around you. But when you know how your brain creates that response, you have the power to create a new one.

We have inherited a brain that's inclined to go negative. It's not that we want to feel bad—on the contrary, our brain evolved to seek good feelings. We go negative because our brain expects negativity to feel good. This paradox makes sense when you know the operating system we've inherited from our animal ancestors. All mammals have the same brain chemicals controlled by the same basic brain structures. Your mammal brain rewards you with good feelings when you do things that promote your survival. But your brain defines survival in a quirky way. This is why we end up with patterns that feel bad in our quest to feel good.

You can transcend your natural mammalian negativity. You can train your brain to go positive. This book shows how to rewire yourself for positivity in six weeks, in just three minutes a day. Positivity does not mean ignoring the realities of life. It means adjusting for the brain's natural tendency to ignore the positives of life. Whether you're frustrated by your own negativity or the negativity of others, *The Science of Positivity* can help.

First, we'll explore the negative and positive chemicals that control your brain. Then you'll learn how to PARE negativity with **P**ersonal

Agency and Realistic Expectations. You can build a positive thought habit that lets in all the good that your inner mammal overlooked.

You may find it hard to believe that there are good things you've missed. It's easy to think your internal responses are caused by external facts because that is what the verbal part of your brain says. But your mammal brain doesn't process language so your two brains are literally not on speaking terms. Your internal responses rest on neural pathways paved by your early neurochemical ups and downs. The electricity in your brain flows into those old pathways unless you carve new ones. This book shows you how to build new pathways and give your electricity a new place to flow!

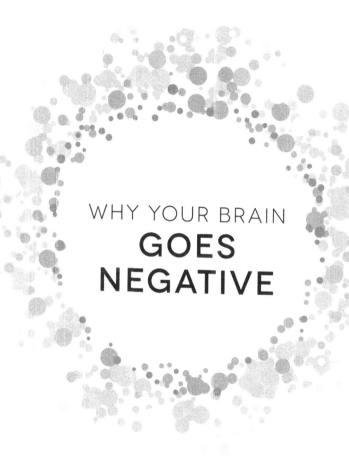

CHAPTER 1

WHY YOUR BRAIN
GOES
NEGATIVE

*Negativity feels good to your old circuits, but
you can build new, positive circuits.*

Do you get a bad feeling when you look at the world around you? Are you surrounded by people who only seem to focus on what's wrong? Do you wish you could enjoy more positive responses but fear that may be unwise or impossible?

Your response to the world is a learned habit. Our habits are hard to notice because they're just physical pathways in the brain. These pathways channel electricity from your information inputs to your positive or negative brain chemicals. Your pathways were built from your unique life experience. The positive and negative experiences of your past paved neural pathways that channel your electricity today.

Negative thought patterns do not mean something is wrong with you. Negativity is natural. The science of positivity shows you why your mammal brain tends to go negative unless you build in a simple adjustment. This book will not tell you what to feel positive about— that's for you to decide—but it will explain how your old pathways got there and how you can build new ones. Anyone can do it!

In this chapter, you'll meet the inner mammal whose ups and downs are explained in depth later on in the book.

OBSERVING YOUR LENS ON LIFE

You may be thinking, "the bad things I see are quite real." But this simple anecdote shows how easily our brain goes negative: Dog poop was a common sidewalk hazard when I was young. It was normal to let your pet mess in public and we couldn't imagine a world in which people routinely cleaned up after their pets. Today, most streets are gloriously free of dog poop. Did that make anyone happy? Not a bit. We rage at the occasional oops instead of noticing the enormity of the accomplishment. Wailing over one "jerk" who fouls the sidewalk seems more normal than celebrating the myriad sanitary successes. This "normal" thought habit does not leave you with a more accurate view of the world. It just leaves you feeling, well, shitty.

You may think anger was necessary to create that change. You may think negativity gives you power. But negativity is often just a habit. Historical perspective helps us see that, so here's a great example. In 1896, the *London Spectator* reported that society would be ruined by the invention of the bicycle. According to the agonizers of the day, the bicycle would end serious conversation by freeing people to flit in and out of more distant social groups instead of lingering for long talks with one group. Meaningful conversation would also be destroyed by the early bedtimes that extra exercise would provoke, it was reported. Behold the human brain at work, busily searching for negatives. You may think you would not have bought into such old rubbish, but you may be buying into new rubbish.

Most people pride themselves on their keen sense of the world's flaws, so it's hard to think of your indictments as a neural network that can simply be replaced. But you see things differently when you understand the operating system we've inherited from our animal ancestors. The brain chemicals that make us feel good (such as dopamine, serotonin, oxytocin, and endorphin) are inherited from earlier mammals. They motivate a mammal to promote its own survival by rewarding survival behaviors with a good feeling. When you know how your happy chemicals work in the state of nature, negativity makes sense. Before we explore that, let's define "negativity."

NEGATIVITY AND CYNICISM

Negative thought patterns come in many varieties, but let's use one very general negative thought pattern for purposes of illustration: cynicism. This habit of thinking "something is wrong with the world" or "it's all going downhill" is widespread. If you do not share this habit, you probably know many who do.

I was sitting in a café in Albania when cynicism suddenly made sense to me. I was being interviewed by an Albanian journalist about my book on resisting bribes. She had a translator with her, and I had a translator with me, so everything we said had to travel through many brains. When I used the word "cynicism," the three Albanians began a flurry of debate. I couldn't understand it, but I heard the word "pessimism" spoken in English.

"No!" I interrupted. "Cynicism is not the same as pessimism!" Then I froze. How could I explain the difference in a way that would survive this tortured communication chain? The answer came to me when I remembered the curious smiles I see on people's faces when they say, "The world is going to hell in a handbasket." Pessimism is distinctly unhappy, but people sound oddly happy when they proclaim their cynicism.

I wanted to know why, so I started discussing cynicism wherever I could. I usually got the same response: "Which kind of cynicism do you mean?" People seem to make a strong distinction between "good" cynicism and "bad" cynicism, but they seem to define good in a way that means "my social allies" and bad in a way that means "my social rivals." So they see cynicism as abhorrent selfishness on the part of "them," but essential realism on the part of "us." This book has no implied "them" or "us." It takes no position on the relative virtue of one group of people or another. That may seem wrong, because we all have strong feelings about the superiority of our own ethics. But this simple thought experiment helps us transcend that.

Imagine you're at an intersection with a four-way stop sign. Another guy rolls through his stop and you think, "That's outrageous! He could have killed someone. Where are the police? What is wrong with this world?" But the next day, you roll through a stop sign. The police are there and you get ticketed. This triggers your cortisol, which lights up the circuits that tell you: "Everybody does it! Why did *I* get punished? The system stinks! What's wrong with this world?"

Confidence in your own righteousness leads to a lose-lose response to this situation, where you feel endangered on the road and wronged by the rules. A positive lens on life would generate a different response. You would notice that traffic laws protect you from harm. You would realize that no enforcement system can catch every violation, but you volunteer for punishment when you choose to violate the rules. You can enjoy the win-win feeling that laws protect you from speeders and controlling your speed protects you from traffic tickets.

You will not see the good if you are looking for the bad. It's natural to look for the bad because the mind doesn't waste energy keeping track of what goes right. We don't appreciate the daily miracle of heavy-metal projectiles passing each other at high speeds in safety. We don't applaud the enforcement system when it runs without bribery, graft, and tribalism. Our minds zero in on threats.

Each brain sees right and wrong through the lens of its survival needs in each moment. We tend to invoke the greater good to explain our own survival efforts, while condemning the efforts of our rivals as "cynical." The good intentions of your social allies seem obvious, and the bad intentions of your social adversaries seem obvious, too. (Psychologists call this "fundamental attribution error.") In this book, we will avoid presumptions about good guys and bad guys to focus on what we have in common: a brain built by natural selection.

YOUR INNER MAMMAL

The mammalian survival system is simple: A chemical that feels good is released when the brain sees something good for its survival, and a chemical that feels bad is released when it sees a survival threat. Positive chemicals motivate a mammal to move toward things that simulate them and negative chemicals motivate a mammal to avoid things that stimulate them. A mammal survives by seeking what feels good and avoiding what feels bad.

The **Mammal Brain** Says . . .

Positive chemicals motivate a mammal to move toward things that stimulate them and negative chemicals motivate a mammal to avoid things that stimulate them.

You may think that you are too evolved to care about your own survival. You may have been told that it's wrong to focus on mere survival. But you think this with your verbal cortex, which does not control your happy chemicals. If you want to feel good, you have to make peace with your mammal brain. That term is used here to refer to the brain structures present in all mammals, including the hippocampus, amygdala, hypothalamus, and the lower parts often called the "reptile brain." All mammals have a cortex too, but size matters when it comes to the cortex. The huge human cortex gives us huge access to associations between past, present, and future. You can draw on these associations as you navigate toward the good and away from the bad. But you cannot ignore your mammal brain. It connects your higher brain to your body, so a neurochemical response from your mammal brain is necessary for action to happen. Our two brains are designed to work together.

Your mammal brain does not report its responses to your cortex in words because words are abstractions and the mammal brain is not designed for abstractions. When you talk to yourself, it's all in your cortex. You can get the idea that your verbal inner voice is the whole story, but a lot more is going on. Animals are constantly making survival decisions without ever putting things into words. Exploring animal behavior helps us understand the positive and negative signals produced by our inner mammal.

Imagine you are a zebra enjoying some juicy green grass. Suddenly, you smell a lion. What do you do? If you run, you miss out on the badly needed food. But if you stay, the bad feeling that surges is much worse than hunger pain. Fortunately, the mammal brain is designed for just such dilemmas. It notices that the lion is a safe distance away. The zebra knows it can eat as long as the lion remains at that distance. So it constantly watches the lion while it eats, and has eyes at the top of its head for just this purpose! We don't have those big eyes, but we have a big cortex to monitor potential threats. Like the hungry zebra, seeing a threat can feel safer than not seeing it. You can easily get into the habit of watching a threat. You feel good when you see the threat because it means you can safely go back to meeting your needs.

You have inherited your brain from individuals who survived. That may sound obvious, but it's almost miraculous when you think about it. Survival rates were low in the state of nature, yet your ancestors, going all the way back, managed to do what it takes to create offspring who survived to create offspring. You've inherited a brain that promotes survival by making it feel good.

Meeting a need feels good, but relieving a threat feels even better. This makes sense because a threat can wipe you out in an instant, but you can usually survive a bit longer without meeting needs. The pleasure of relieving a bad feeling is huge, whether it's escaping from a criminal or finding your cell phone. It's not surprising that threats get priority in our brain.

Good feelings mask your sense of threat, but they are not designed to be "on" all the time. Good feelings evolved to turn on in short spurts when you do something to meet a need. Then they turn off and you have to do more to get more. When a happy chemical spurt ends, potential threats get your attention again. It may feel like something is wrong, even though your brain is just resetting to neutral. If you recognize the happy chemical droop as nature's reset, you know it's not a crisis. But if you expect your happy chemicals to surge all the time, you will feel like something is wrong a lot. You may feel an urgent need to "do something" to make it stop. You may even rush into something that leaves you less safe in the long run. You are much better off knowing your happy chemicals are meant to alert you to things that promote survival rather than to flow for no reason.

The mammal brain defines survival in a quirky way, alas, and that makes life complicated. Your inner mammal cares about the survival of your genes (even though you don't consciously think that), and it relies on the neural pathways you built in youth. This makes sense in the state of nature, where things that feel good are good for the survival of your genes. But a mammal is not born with the survival skills of its ancestors. It builds the pathways that turn its neurochemicals on and off with each experience. By the time a young mammal's elders are gone, it has the neural network it needs to meets its needs.

HOW YOUR NEURAL NETWORK GOT BUILT

Humans are born with billions of neurons but very few connections between them. We build those connections from life experience, starting from the moment of conception. We don't need to remember those experiences for them to have power over us. The electricity in your brain flows like water in a storm, finding the path of least resistance. Good and bad feelings are like paving on your neural pathways. Whatever felt good or bad in your past connected all the neurons active at that moment. Now, electricity can rush down that pathway and tell you how to get more of those good feelings or avoid whatever caused the bad feelings.

Whatever felt good or bad in your past connected all the neurons active at that moment. Now, electricity can rush down that pathway and tell you how to get more of those good feelings or avoid whatever caused the bad feelings.

Some neural pathways become the superhighways of your brain, thanks to a substance called "myelin." It coats neurons the way insulation coats a wire, allowing electricity to flow at super speeds. Anything you do with myelinated neurons feels natural and easy. Anything you do with unmyelinated neurons feels labored and uncertain. Myelin is abundant in your brain before age 8, and during puberty. Thus, you end up looking at the world through a lens shaped in high school, and so does everyone else. You add to it, of course, but we tend to add leaves to our neural trees rather than replace the branches. When you look at the world through your myelinated lens, you can often end up feeling like something is wrong.

THE PROBLEM WITH HAPPY CHEMICALS

Your happy brain chemicals are always going up and down. That's how they do their job. When they go up, you feel like your needs will be met and all is right with the world. But when they droop, you feel like you will be in big trouble unless you do something urgently. Here's a quick look at what turns on each of the happy chemicals, and why they naturally droop after they spurt.

Dopamine

The excitement of dopamine is released when you expect to meet a need. Your prehistoric ancestors had to forage constantly to survive, and dopamine made it feel good. When your ancestors saw a tree full of ripe berries in the distance, their dopamine surged and they moved toward it. Dopamine releases energy when a reward is expected, and it also connects neurons that tell you how to find more of the reward in the future.

But finding a berry tree didn't make your ancestors feel good forever. Their dopamine drooped when they reached the tree because it had already done its job. The brain doesn't waste dopamine on old information. Your ancestors had to find a new way to meet a need to enjoy more dopamine. Life is challenging because our brain takes what you have for granted and saves the dopamine for "new and improved." You may blame this on "our society." I did that and so did everyone around me. But when you understand the mammal brain, you can build realistic expectations. Otherwise, you are likely to think something is wrong with the world every time your dopamine droops.

Oxytocin

The good feeling of oxytocin is released when you find social support. Mammals seek safety in numbers because oxytocin makes it feel good. But life in a herd of mammals is not all warm and fuzzy. Your herd-mates often get in the way of the food or mating opportunity you have your eye on. If you leave them, your oxytocin falls and your cortisol surges. You feel like something very bad is about to happen. In the state of nature, this motivated animals to stick with the herd and avoid instant death in the jaws of a predator. Today, it causes anxiety when you think you lack social support. You can relieve that anxiety by attaching yourself to one herd or another, but it often fails to feel as good as you expect. So you end up frustrated when you're with a herd and frustrated when you're not. You imagine a better herd that makes you feel safe all the time, but you never seem to find it. It feels like something is wrong with the world. But when you understand your inner mammal, you can build realistic expectations about oxytocin droop.

Serotonin

The good feeling of serotonin is released when you find a way to get ahead. You may blame competitive urges on "our society," but hierarchical behavior is part of every animal's daily life. Living in groups forces weaker mammals and stronger ones to live side by side. When one sees a juicy bit of food or a mating opportunity, another sees it too. Natural selection built a brain that constantly compares itself to others. If a mammal sees that it's weaker than the individual next to it, it restrains itself to avoid the pain of conflict. If a mammal sees that it's stronger than the individual next to it, serotonin is released and it feels good. Serotonin is not aggression, but the nice feeling that it's safe to act on the urge to meet your needs.

Each serotonin spurt is quickly metabolized, however, so the brain is always looking for another way to stimulate the good feeling. Getting the one-up position helped a mammal spread its genes. In the modern world, we are not trying to spread our genes. We struggle to find ways to enjoy serotonin without the harmful consequences of being seen as "a jerk." Feeling morally superior to others is a popular solution. But the serotonin you stimulate is soon processed and you have to feel superior again to get more. If you don't understand the brain's natural urge for social dominance, you are likely to feel that something is wrong with the world.

Endorphin

The good feeling of endorphin is released when you experience physical pain. It's often associated with "runner's high," but runners only get it if they run to the point of pain. Endorphin masks pain with a good feeling, which enables an injured mammal to do what it takes to seek safety. The endorphin soon passes because pain is vital information. It tells you not to touch a hot stove or run on a broken leg. Endorphin evolved for emergencies, not for us to inflict pain on ourselves to enjoy it. Anyone who seeks it discovers that the brain habituates and it takes more and more pain to feel good. This is a very bad survival strategy. We are better off just being glad to have it for emergencies. But humans find various ways to seek endorphin, and tragedy often results. Endorphin is not further addressed in this book because we are not meant to stimulate it intentionally.

WHAT ABOUT CORTISOL?

Pain is caused by cortisol. In the modern world, cortisol is known as the "stress chemical." Stress is the anticipation of pain from your inner mammal's perspective. A small brain makes the small link between the smell of a lion and the pain of a lion's jaws. A big brain can anticipate a huge range of inputs leading to potential future pain. Social pain is produced in the mammal brain when it sees a potential future threat to meeting its social needs. When your world is relatively free of physical pain, social pain gets your attention.

Cortisol is nature's emergency broadcast system. Neurons connect when cortisol flows, so anything that ever caused you pain built a neural pathway in your brain. That makes it easy to turn on the cortisol alarm when you see anything similar in the future. A big brain can see similarities in huge clusters of detail. You can end up with a lot of cortisol, even in a rather good life. It motivates you to scan urgently for ways to relieve it. Whatever relieved your cortisol in the past connected neurons that trigger expectations of relief in your future.

Telling yourself, "something is wrong with the world" brings surprising relief. It helps relieve cortisol by offering a threat to monitor. It stimulates your serotonin, as you feel superior to those who fail to get it. It stimulates your oxytocin by helping you bond with those who share your concern. It stimulates your dopamine by helping you focus on new rewards. Alas, the good feelings are soon metabolized and you have to feel bad about the world again to stimulate more. You can easily wire in the habit.

WIRING YOURSELF FOR POSITIVITY

When you have a sense of crisis, it feels like external evidence is the cause. But when you know the internal causes of negativity, you can create positivity instead. A simple method for doing that is presented in Chapter 6. It shows how to PARE your negativity with **P**ersonal

Agency and **R**ealistic **E**xpectations. Personal Agency is the awareness that you can meet your real needs through your own actions. Realistic Expectations are the knowledge that rewards are unpredictable, and frustration is not a survival threat. When you PARE, you will REAP, because **R**ealistic **E**xpectations lead to **A**cting **P**ersonally. With realistic expectations about the brain chemistry we've inherited, you act personally to meet your needs instead of expecting the world to meet them for you. You don't always get what you seek, but you enjoy being your own agent instead of lamenting the world's failure to meet your expectations.

Chapter 6 provides a simple exercise that takes 3 minutes a day and will rewire you in six weeks. You can start today. You don't have to wait for the world to change. You don't have to wait for the people around you to approve. You only have to focus on the good all around you until your electricity has a new place to flow. Chapter 7 helps you see what the world looks like when you take off the crisis goggles.

I had a great positivity experience at the Valley of Monkeys (La Vallée des Singes in France). It was feeding time at the mandrills, and a keeper was explaining how the female mandrill strives to mate with the male whose colors are brightest. Male mandrills have rainbow-striped fur on their faces and derrière. They can't control their fur color directly but their bodies evolved to produce brighter colors when they dominate their group-mates. The harsh facts of animal competitiveness are uncomfortable for many people. You might prefer to imagine nature as pristine and egalitarian. It's painful to think of drab gray males sitting around watching the more colorful guys get all the action. It's sad to think of female mandrills ending up alone because they've all gone for the same guy. But there was a big positive behind this. I asked the keeper about mandrills' relationship to baboons because I noticed many similarities. She said that mandrills are less violent. Baboons compete for females with direct physical conflict, but mandrills rarely engage in physical violence because they compete on appearances. What a fabulous insight! When competition over appearances frustrates us in daily life, it's great to know that appearances are an evolved substitute for violence.

The keeper explained that wild mandrills have much brighter colors than the ones we see at the zoo. In the wild, mandrills live in large groups where competition is more intense than in small groups. This stimulates more hormones, which leads to more dramatic sexual signaling. The females are as much a part of this competitiveness as the males. Stronger females strive to get better genes for their children who will thus have brighter fur and make more copies of mom's genes. Of course, mandrills don't think conceptually about conception. They just do what it takes to stimulate happy chemicals in the brain built by natural selection.

You may condemn all competition with your verbal brain, but your inner mammal cares about your survival. With realistic expectations, you would see that it's normal for others to have the same desires that you have. If you want the room with the view, it's not surprising that others want it, too. You may deride those who strive for the "good room" while overlooking your own striving for it.

Condemning the world around you is a waste of your energy. A mandrill doesn't waste energy condemning "the system," though its life is far harsher than yours. If you were a male mandrill, your fur would be judged all the time and you would need to jockey for social status to stimulate those hormones. As a modern human, you get to choose when and how you compete. You can view mammalian social rivalry through the lens of Personal Agency and Realistic Expectations. You can PARE your cynicism and feel good in the world as it is!

Cynicism is pervasive in the world around us. People insist that things are bad and getting worse. They say our leaders are bad, our culture is bad, our health is bad, our species is bad, our planet is going downhill, the last century was the worst ever, and this millennium is already shaping up to be a bad one. When I hear this, I remind myself that the brain goes negative because it expects that to feel good.

Science Summary

The mammal brain promotes survival by looking for ways to stimulate positive brain chemicals and avoid negative brain chemicals.

- Your positive brain chemicals (dopamine, serotonin, oxytocin) motivate you to seek things that stimulate them. Your negative brain chemical (cortisol) motivates you to avoid things that stimulate it.

- Happy chemicals are not meant to be on all the time. They're released when you meet a need. Then they droop and you have to do more to get more.

- Neurons connect when your brain chemicals flow, which wires you to seek things that stimulated your happy chemicals before and avoid things that stimulated your cortisol.

- Relief from threat is the brain's top priority. Anything that relieved a threat in your past built a pathway that triggers positive expectations about similar cues for the future.

- All mammals have the same brain chemicals managed by the same core brain structures.

- Humans also have a large cortex than enables us to manipulate abstractions, such as words. The mammal brain does not process language and does not report in words why it turns the chemicals on and off.

- Negativity feels good when old pathways connect it to the expectation of happy chemicals or the relief of cortisol.

- Myelin insulates neurons the way plastic insulates wires, transforming some neural circuits into superhighways with huge processing speed (like optical fiber as compared to old-fashioned copper wire). The neural networks you myelinated in youth tell you instantly what is good for you and what isn't. The world makes sense effortlessly when information flows through your myelinated circuits.

- The electricity in your brain flows like water in a storm, finding the paths of least resistance. Your electricity will keep using old pathways unless you build new ones.

- Personal Agency is the awareness that you can meet your real needs through your own actions. Realistic Expectations are the knowledge that rewards are unpredictable, and frustration is not a survival threat. You can PARE your negativity and enjoy the act of meeting needs instead of lamenting the world's failure to meet them for you.

CHAPTER 2

THE POSITIVITY OF
ESCAPING
THREATS

*Escaping a threat feels good,
which motivates you to repeat
behaviors that create the good feeling.*

Nothing promotes survival like escaping a threat, so nothing feels as good.

Cortisol evolved to make you feel awful, so anything that stops the flow of cortisol feels good. Fighting, fleeing, freezing, and fawning stop threats in the state of nature, and they feel good. (Fawning is the mammalian strategy of avoiding harm by submitting to social dominance.)

Negativity is a way of fighting, fleeing, freezing, or fawning. These thought patterns help us escape a sense of threat, so they feel good. When the good feeling stops, you can always repeat them. Unfortunately, you have to keep feeling bad about the world in order to keep enjoying these good feelings.

This chapter shows how your unhappy chemical creates a sense of crisis, and how we build habits to get relief. Those habits sometimes add to our sense of crisis, but we have power over them when we know where they come from.

THE JOY OF RELIEVING UNHAPPY CHEMICALS

Your brain evolved in a world full of threat, so escaping from threat became Job #1. Once your cortisol turns on, anything that turns it off, even for just a moment, feels good. The famous fight-or-flight response turns off cortisol, which is why it's so pervasive. We are used to thinking of this response as a bad thing, but it helps to know that fighting and fleeing are the tools a mammal has to escape from threat. It feels good to fight or flee, compared to the horror of doing nothing in the face of threat.

When we humans feel threatened, we too feel an urgent need to "do something" to relieve the threat. Our big cortex helps us analyze lots of detail about our options. We realize that fighting has consequences. We notice that fleeing has consequences. A big brain can improve its prospects by fighting or fleeing abstractly. Negativity is a way to fight or flee without the physical actions. Negativity makes it possible to fight without physical harm, and to flee without running away. Anything that makes a bad feeling stop feels great.

Neurons connect when our neurochemicals flow, so if negativity relieves a bad feeling, we expect more relief from more negativity. If you gain a moment's relief when you tell yourself "isn't it always that way," you wire yourself to say "isn't it always that way" again.

HOW THE BRAIN CONSTRUCTS A THREAT

You've probably heard the expression "I smell trouble." It's a great reminder of the fact that trouble is information we take in through our senses. A zebra feels threatened because the lion molecules that reached its nose triggered neurons that sent electricity to its cortisol. A zebra does not feel threatened because it has a cognitive concept of being eaten alive by neighbors who will always be there. It doesn't have enough neurons for abstraction. It is not interested in philosophical generalizations about the state of the world. It is only interested in doing something to make the cortisol stop. And the first step for doing that is to take in more information about the threat. In a moment of crisis, the zebra's brain skillfully zooms in on evidence of the lion's whereabouts, and screens out other data.

We mammals are always looking for information that can help us escape harm. The big human cortex is especially good at scanning for evidence of threat. We have ten times more neurons going from our brain to our eyes than we have from our eyes to our brain. That means we are ten times more equipped to find the information we're looking for than to process whatever happens to come along. Once our cortisol turns on, we are very good at finding threat signals.

But what turns on the cortisol? In the modern world, it's not the smell of lions.

Cortisol, the unhappy chemical, evolved to signal physical pain. You may be surprised to learn that pain is valuable information. It motivates you to take your hand off a hot stove, fast. You don't have to touch a hot stove twice because the brain stores everything going on while cortisol flows. You immediately learn to avoid anything resembling that hot stove. This ability to store and retrieve experience rests on a chemical called acetylcholine. It triggers the "remember what happened the last time you did that" feeling. Adrenaline adds the sense that something is ultra-urgent. If you decide to walk over hot coals, a surge of adrenaline alerts you to the very high stakes. Adrenaline and acetylcholine respond to good things as well as bad things, such as a glance from a special someone or a delicious smell. They rev your engine for action, but cortisol tells your engine to avoid rather than approach. Cortisol is the chemical that distinguishes bad-excited from good-excited.

Cortisol is found in lizards, frogs, fish, mollusks, and even amoeba. It promotes survival by causing such a bad feeling that an organism stops doing other things to focus on relieving it. The brain learns from pain, but a small brain only learns to avoid a hot stove that's just like the hot stove that caused the pain. A big brain activates a big web of circuits so the individual learns to avoid anything vaguely similar to a hot stove.

When a brain sees something that caused pain before, electricity flows to the cortisol switch and alerts the body in time to avoid it. Avoiding pain is a much better survival strategy than trying to escape once you're in it. For example:

- A gazelle would not survive if it had to feel the pain of a lion's jaws before it felt threatened.
- A lion would not survive if it had to feel the pain of starvation before it started hunting.
- Your ancestor would not have survived if they waited for the pain of frozen toes before they started stocking firewood.

We mammals survive by anticipating pain and acting to avoid it. Our cortisol alarm helps us do that.

Cortisol's New Job

Mammals evolved a new job for cortisol: social pain. The link between physical pain and social pain is clear in the mammal world. Isolation can lead to the pain of a predator's jaws. But being near others can also lead to painful bites and scratches from troop-mates if you approach their food. Each painful experience of isolation or conflict wires a mammal to release more cortisol in similar situations. That's why hurt feelings trigger the same chemical as physical hurt. In a social animal, social threats feel as urgent as physical threats.

Hurt feelings trigger the same chemical as physical hurt. In a social animal, both are relevant to survival.

The bigger a mammal's brain, the more social threats it can anticipate. Anything similar to past hurtful encounters can get your cortisol going. You can feel endangered a lot of the time, even though you consciously know the difference between physical pain and social pain. Cortisol creates a sense of urgency that's hard to ignore. Humans attach words to the cortisol feeling. We call it fear, anxiety, stress, panic, shame, dread, suffering, misery, unhappiness, or pain, depending on the quantity and the context. In every case, the underlying message is "make it stop!"

RUNNING FROM PAIN

Animals respond to cortisol with action rather than words. They fight, flee, freeze, or fawn, because these behaviors can stop threats. Understanding these animal responses sheds light on our own responses to cortisol. We'll see eerie parallels between negativity and the animal impulse to fight, flee, freeze, or fawn. In a moment when you feel threatened, negative thoughts can feel good.

To the mammal brain, anything that relieves cortisol promotes survival. So if a cigarette relieved your anxiety one day, your mammal brain "learned" that cigarettes promote survival. If pizza relieved a sense of threat in your youth, your mammal brain learned that pizza promotes survival. If cynicism helps you experience cortisol relief, your brain learns to see it as a lifesaver. No one thinks this in words, of course. But in a moment when your cortisol surges and you look for a way to make it stop, your brain relies on the neural circuits it has. These circuits can associate cynicism with relief as automatically as they associate water with relief of thirst or a warm fire with relief of chill.

When you see a lizard basking in the sun, you may think it's feeling good, but it is living in crisis. It risks being eaten alive every moment it lingers out in the open. But if it runs under a rock, it risks dying of hypothermia. So a lizard only basks in the sun when it feels like it's dying of cold, and it stays on high alert the whole time. As soon as its body temperature reaches the safe zone, it rushes back into hiding and stays there until it feels like it's dying of hunger or cold again. A lizard is always running from pain. It survives by skillfully choosing which threat is most urgent at each moment.

Every mammal has a reptile brain at its core because evolution builds on what's already there. We humans have inherited the same brain structures that enable a lizard to choose between one life-threatening risk and another. At the back of your neck, where your spine meets your brain (the cerebellum, medulla oblongata, and pons, often called the "brain stem"), you have structures that alert you to threats and prompt action that keeps you alive. This "reptile brain" manages metabolic functions like breathing and digesting as well as responding to danger. A reptile also has a tiny hippocampus and hypothalamus to process new inputs into decisions. Your hippocampus and hypothalamus are more sophisticated and can process more inputs, but they connect with your brain stem to interpret threats just like a lizard's does. We humans also have a huge reserve of extra neurons, but they feed information down into our reptile brain to connect to the rest of our body in order to take action. So all of our complex analysis distills down to a go or no-go. We may strategize and optimize profusely, but we boil it all down to the act of approaching what we expect to help and avoiding what we expect to hurt.

The **Reptile Brain** Says . . .

I scan for threats. It's always a crisis. I escape, and then find the next closest threat.

The reptile brain has gotten a bad reputation. You may have been told to avoid "reptilian thinking," but you cannot shut off your reptile brain. It's the base of your operating system. You are better off understanding it. It is always trying to protect you from harm by detecting threats in time to avoid them. That said, the reptile brain can get quirky ideas about threats. It can create the feeling that you will die if you don't have a cigarette or a pizza, or the feeling that cynicism protects you from hurt. The reptilian response to cynicism does not rest on erudite socioeconomic analysis. It rests on the pathways you built in the past.

We don't act on every quirky reptilian impulse, of course. But we can't just ignore these impulses because the reptile brain thinks survival is at stake. It escalates when you ignore it. "Do something! Do something!" it keeps telling you. To stop the cortisol from flowing, you must satisfy your inner reptile.

MAKE IT STOP

The first step to stopping cortisol is identifying the threat. Cortisol can warn of internal threats, like hunger, or external ones, like predators. Your brain has to figure out what turned it on in order to turn it off. For example, when low blood sugar turns on a lizard's cortisol, eating makes it stop. So a lizard looks for food when it gets the painful feeling we call "hunger." But when your hand is on a hot stove, food doesn't relieve pain. And avoiding hot stoves doesn't relieve hunger pain. You have to interpret your cortisol in order to survive. A small brain does that with a small number of circuits. A big brain has so many circuits that the do-something feeling can be hard to make sense of. Fortunately, we have acetylcholine to say "remember!" and adrenaline to say "now!"

Lizards succeed at relieving cortisol, but the bad feeling soon returns. Hunger returns once food is digested. Predators return once you escape from them. The brain is always busy scanning for the next potential source of harm. A small brain focuses on immediate threats instead of worrying about tomorrow's hunger or lasting peace with predators. It has just enough neural horsepower to seek immediate relief from immediate threats.

Reptiles have a smidgeon of cortex, too, so they have a limited ability to learn. They learn from pain. When a lizard feels the pain of an eagle's talon in its sides, a surge of cortisol connects all the neurons active at that moment. If the lizard survives the encounter, it is now wired to detect an eagle faster the next time because the sight and smell of an eagle built bridges between activated neurons. Experience augments the predator-avoidance circuits that a lizard is born with.

A lizard doesn't "know" what an eagle is. It simply avoids sensory inputs that trigger cortisol. A lizard runs for cover when it sees the sudden shadow caused by an eagle overhead. Reptiles evolved a life-style that requires very few neurons. This promotes survival because neurons burn a lot of fuel. The efficient reptile operating system works by avoiding things that feel bad without asking why.

SOCIAL PAIN

Reptiles have no social life. They leave home the instant they're born, and their parents eat them if they don't leave fast enough. With no chance to learn from their elders, they are born hardwired with just enough skills to survive. A huge percentage of young reptiles are eaten by predators before they reach puberty, but their species survive because they make babies by the thousands.

Mammals can't do that because a warm-blooded baby is much harder to gestate than a cold-blooded baby. Mammals put all their eggs in very few baskets, so their genes can easily get wiped out. To survive, they protect their young from predators with strong social bonds.

Reptiles don't have social pain because they don't need other reptiles to survive. In fact, reptiles can't stand being near each other, and avoid their colleagues except while mating. But mammals evolved a brain that enjoys company, and even feels threatened without it. Cortisol surges when a mammal is separated from its group, making separation feel like a survival emergency.

But living in a group is not easy. When a mammal sees food, other group-mates see it too. When a mammal lunges at food, it may get a painful kick or scratch from a herd-mate. The mammal brain strives to avoid the pain of conflict while also avoiding the pain of hunger and the pain of social isolation. It performs this balancing act with circuits built from experience.

Reptiles are born prewired with the experience of their ancestors, but mammals wire themselves from their own life experience. We mammals connect our neurons by interacting with the world around us. We have time to do that because we are protected from harm during an early period of dependency. Of course, each young mammal must learn to avoid harm once its mother is gone in order for the species to survive. Each mammal learns from its own good and bad experiences.

Learning from experience has drawbacks. If you had to learn about lions by getting bitten, few mammals would survive their first lesson. Instead, mammals developed a capacity for social learning. If a young zebra wanders too far from the herd, its mother bites it and the pain quickly teaches the youngster to associate wandering off with pain. Hunger pain also grows during separation from the mother. A young brain can learn to link separation and pain before it comes to harm.

Mammals also have mirror neurons that sense the pleasure and pain of others. A lost baby senses its mother's panic when they reunite. A young mammal senses the panic of its herd-mates when a predator approaches. Mirroring builds a young brain's connections between separation and cortisol, and between companionship and relief. Mirroring helps a young mammal learn the behaviors that others use to escape threat. Thus, social learning helps a human brain learn the negativity of those around it.

The **Reptile Brain** Says . . .

Reptiles avoid their colleagues except while mating.

NEGATIVITY IN ACTION

A threatened mammal is designed to act fast. Fight and flight are well-known responses, but freezing and fawning are equally important. A close look at each of these strategies is useful because they are a mammal's threat-relief tool kit. We will see how the human brain can accomplish each of them with negativity and cynicism.

Fight

The natural response to threat is to withdraw, but fighting is the opposite. You approach whatever threatens you. Big-brained humans can fight with words as well as with physical conflict. We can even fight with words that are highly abstract. For example, when you feel threatened you may berate "the idiots in power" instead of directly fighting with an individual. We learn to curb our aggression and find other ways to enjoy the powerful feeling of approaching a perceived threat.

Fighting might seem like a cause of distress, but when a mammal is attacked, fighting back can relieve distress. Of course, a physical fight comes with the risk of injury and pain, which is why animals only fight as a last resort, or when they're sure they can win. In the human world, a verbal fight can also lead to injury and pain, which is why it's so tempting to fight with generalized cynicism like "they're all morons." When you feel attacked, you may find yourself venting with such abstractions, and it may actually bring relief in the moment. If you do this repeatedly, however, you are likely to augment the neural pathways that make you feel attacked.

Sometimes you have to fight. Imagine a mother lion that hasn't eaten for days. When she finally catches a gazelle, hyenas swoop in to steal it. Should she fight them? If she loses the fight, her children are likely to perish. But if she doesn't fight, her milk will dry up and her children will starve. She doesn't think this in words. Her electricity simply flows through the circuits she has. Cortisol surges as she anticipates the pain of fighting but it also surges as she anticipates the pain of not fighting. One circuit triggers less cortisol, so it feels good in relative terms. When fighting feels better than fleeing, her adrenaline and testosterone surge and she rushes toward the threat instead of running away from it.

Mammals fight when they expect to gain more than they lose. A big gain is expected whenever reproduction is involved, whether it's protecting a child from harm or prevailing over rivals for mating opportunity. Fights usually begin with what biologists call "display," which is triggered by the intent to fight. A mammal shows its weapons and puffs up its size to encourage the adversary to back down. This often works, which is why people say, "it's just for show." But there is always a chance that the adversary will attack instead of backing down, so a mammal who displays must be prepared to fight.

Mammals choose their battles carefully. Research shows that animals only fight when they expect to win. They are skilled at assessing their own strength in comparison to others. They build this skill in youth through play and by watching their parents decide when to fight and when to retreat to safety. A young mammal at play is testing its strength against others. Brains that chose badly were weeded out by natural selection, so a brain skilled at making social comparisons evolved. Social comparison is a core survival skill.

In the modern world, we learn that fighting is wrong whether or not you can win. If your child fights over a cookie, you are likely to punish the child and take away the cookie. You may think your fine words are instructive, but the child's brain learns from the cookie. If the child gets to keep the ill-gotten treat, his brain learns that fighting gets rewards, even if your words suggest otherwise.

Humans learn to fight without physical aggression. Put-downs, lawsuits, and competition (friendly and otherwise) are nonviolent ways to go toward a perceived threat instead of avoiding it. The brain keeps weighing the risk of fighting against the risk of not fighting. Cynicism is a low-risk way to fight. You can say, "They're all jerks" without risking too much pain. You can mentally oppose all men, or all women, or all bosses, or all rich people, or all gluten-eaters. You can rage at public figures when you see them on screens. You can fight city hall. When this relieves your sense of threat, even if just for a moment, the good feeling builds a pathway. The next time you feel bad, that pathway offers you a way to do something. Of course, we don't think that consciously, but when we feel attacked, we say, "They're all jerks" and enjoy the relief.

Conflict is part of a mammal's life. Animals resolve their conflicts without violence much of the time because one individual backs down to avoid injury. But they are at the edge of conflict a lot. We are distracted from this fact by heartwarming stories of animal cooperation, but animals don't expect life to be conflict-free. When a threat triggers their cortisol, they look for a way to promote survival.

For example, stronger monkeys often grab food from weaker troop-mates. You won't see a fight because weaker individuals back down to avoid getting bitten or scratched. Backing down means hunger, weakness, and reproductive failure, so a monkey is always weighing one potential pain against another. The pain of fighting is significant because injuries are often fatal in the wild. They slow you down enough for a predator to pick you off. A monkey may prefer to go hungry today and live to eat tomorrow, but tomorrow's banana may get swiped, too. So a monkey has no choice but to constantly scan for opportunities to prevail, as much as it would rather avoid conflict. If he gets the banana, he feels good.

You may recoil at the idea of fighting weaker individuals. Yet if your boss adds to your workload, you may look for a weaker person to push the task onto. And you may be surprised to find yourself venting at a powerless stranger when you're afraid to stand up to a bully in your home. It takes frontal lobes to anticipate consequences. Monkeys have small frontal lobes but humans have big ones. That's why we spend so much time analyzing alternative scenarios instead of fighting. But as soon as you decide not to fight, it may seem like another monkey is eyeing your banana again. Cynicism is a welcome relief.

Flight

Fleeing is often the best survival strategy. Animals are so aware of this that they constantly scan for escape routes and refuse to enter an enclosed space. Flight is not just for the weak, since stronger animals can get away faster than weaker ones.

Escaping a threat feels good. When a baboon is threatened by a lion, climbing a tree feels good. The baboon does not think, "What is wrong with this world?" or "Tomorrow the lion may be back." It is just glad to have escaped the threat in that moment. It is even happier when the lion leaves so it can climb down the tree and meet its needs. The good feeling wires the baboon to scan for trees when it feels threatened.

We humans can generate abstract images of future threats instead of just worrying about threats within striking distance. We have the amazing ability to activate neurons internally instead of just waiting for the external world to trigger our senses. This enables us to act in time to prevent harm, but it can also leave us with an endless threatened feeling. That's why we're so eager for ways to escape.

Distraction works. Distraction does not protect you from an actual predator, but when an internal image has triggered your cortisol, shifting to a different image interrupts it. This is why distractions of every variety are so popular, even when they have negative consequences.

To complicate things further, cortisol remains in your body for a couple of hours after you stop releasing it. So your sense of alarm continues and keeps you hyper-alert for threats until your body has finished metabolizing it. A big brain can keep finding evidence of threats when it looks. You can get into a bad loop unless you "do something" to stop it. At such times, you scan for past escape tools, the way a baboon scans for a tree. Negativity is activated if it worked for you before. Worrying about the world "going to hell in a handbasket" can distract you from an annoying situation closer to home. Ruminating on the state of the world may not sound like an escape, but it can shift your attention away from threats that are up-close and personal.

Each thought of "the global mess" interrupts more painful thoughts about a personal mess. From your mammal brain's perspective, thoughts of global crisis actually save you from harm. Like running up a tree, it feels good.

Very small cues can trigger the threat alarm of a very big brain. Your boss's raised eyebrow can trigger your cortisol. Fighting is a bad option. Fleeing is a bad option. Running away in your mind may seem like the best option. People can escape by overindulging in food, alcohol, drugs, sex, shopping, screen-watching, and many other habits. Negativity allows you to run away in your mind without the harmful side effects of food, alcohol, drugs, sex, shopping, and gaming. However, people often combine negativity with other escape behaviors. "The world is going to hell, so why not have another cookie/drink/pill/affair/splurge?"

Freeze

A gazelle has the ability to freeze in the presence of a lion. It freezes so completely that the lion may take it for dead. This can promote survival because the lion is inclined to return to its pride to alert them to the meal, at which point the undead gazelle jumps up and escapes. This is a very risky strategy but in desperate circumstances it can work. Freezing is a real physiological response to a huge cortisol spike. It slows a mammal's metabolism so much that its breathing isn't heard. If the animal survives, it is equipped to unfreeze by shaking until the tension is released.

The expression "a deer in headlights" implies that freezing is foolish. But the reflex did not evolve in a world of cars. It evolved in a world of predators, where avoiding notice can save your life. Freezing is dangerous, but it's a way to do something when other options are closed.

Cynicism can be a way of freezing. The mind's equivalent of a freeze response is telling yourself, "The way things are these days, there's nothing I can do." If all the options in front of you look bad, cynical freezing can give you the good feeling of doing something. When you tell yourself, "What can you do in a world like this?" you might feel a moment of relief. That good feeling tells your brain that this way of avoiding harm works, which wires you to repeat the negative thought in another cortisol-drenched moment. The neural pathway grows, and soon you slip easily into the idea that you are frozen because of "the way things are these days."

Fawn

Fawning is another mammalian threat-reliever. Animals submit to more dominant group-mates to protect themselves from threat. In humans, this has been called the "fawn response."

For example, weaker monkeys approach stronger ones with head and eyes down. This signals the intent to submit, and protects a weaker monkey from aggression. Subordinate monkeys often groom the fur of dominant monkeys as well. When fawning relieves a perceived threat, it feels good. You may think such hierarchical behavior is an evil of civilization, but mammals have been dominating and submitting for millions of years. An animal that dominates group-mates gets more of what it takes to spread its genes, such as food, mating opportunities, and protection from predators. Natural selection produced a brain that promotes survival by seeking social dominance . . . but it also knows when to promote survival by fawning to dominance-seekers.

The **Mammal Brain** Says . . .

Natural selection produced a brain that promotes survival by seeking social dominance . . . but it also knows when to promote survival by fawning to dominance-seekers.

The dominance/submission rituals of animals are well known to farmers, zookeepers, and field biologists. When an animal thinks it is stronger than the group-mate in front of it, it makes a dominance gesture, such as a direct stare and puffing of the chest. It expects a submission gesture in return, such as crouched shoulders and lowered eyes. Each animal in a herd or pack or troop knows its own strength relative to each group-mate, and avoids pain by submitting to stronger individuals. By adulthood, each mammal has learned the gestures needed to protect itself from in-group aggression. Fawning does not get you the banana or the mate, but it gets you the peace necessary to meet your needs for another day.

This facet of nature makes people uncomfortable. In fact, many experts are trying to disguise it as "cooperation." It is true that dominant mammals sometimes cooperate by protecting their mates from third-party aggression. But most of the time, they put themselves first, and weaker individuals must "cooperate" with them, or else.

Fawning is easy to see among human primates. Let's say you are threatened by a neighborhood bully, and you find yourself being extra nice to them. You reward the bully in ways you don't reward people who are actually nice to you. This works, from your mammal brain's perspective. It relieves the threat. You can blame your fawning on the system by telling yourself that the bully is just a product of "the system." But your fawning is part of the system that creates the bully.

You are cynically fawning if you give someone money, knowing she will spend it on drugs. You are cynically fawning if someone steals your wallet and you say, "He probably needs it more than I do." If you bribe a corrupt official or pay protection money to a criminal, it's cynical fawning. In each case, you submit for the pleasure of relieving your own threatened feeling. Your verbal cortex finds a reason to act in a way that your mammal brain feels good about. You don't intend to fawn. But in the moment you feel threatened, doing something that relieves the threat feels good. That nice feeling of relief connects neurons, wiring you to fawn again the next time you feel threatened.

You don't "believe" in fawning. You also don't "believe" in fighting, fleeing, or freezing. But when a cortisol surge tells you "something is wrong," you want to make it stop.

BORN FRAGILE

"This is not me," you may say. "I don't fawn or freeze or flee or fight to feel good." "I am no monkey or lion or gazelle." It's easy to think our threat responses are motivated by the intellectual arguments we're so good at producing. To make sense of our threat circuits, we need to trace their development to the beginning.

We humans are far more helpless and vulnerable at birth than our animal ancestors. We enter the world with a more unfinished brain, so we're dependent and needy for much longer than other animals. The first experience in each human life is cortisol, triggered by urgent survival needs you cannot do something about. This sense of threat is at the core of your neurochemical navigator.

A newborn responds to cortisol by crying. It's one of our few prewired behaviors. Over time, you learned alternative ways to respond to cortisol. Each time you succeeded at relieving a threatened feeling, you learned from that experience. You do not consciously remember this learning, but you ended up with lots of circuits for relieving your cortisol.

We often think our early circuits are unimportant because they don't speak to us in grand terms that make us proud. Yet these early circuits are the core of our self-management system. The larger an animal's brain, the more it relies on learned circuits instead of on inborn circuits. The larger an animal's brain, the longer its childhood, because these circuits take so long to build. We humans wire ourselves by interacting with the world instead of being born hardwired with the experience of our ancestors. This allows each new baby to wire itself for present realities instead of relying on what worked in the past. This opportunity took hundreds of millions of years to evolve, so it is foolish to think we just discard our early learning.

A big brain actually makes it harder to survive because neurons need so much glucose, oxygen, and warmth. A big brain only promotes survival if it is wired in a way that gives a critter its money's worth from all those extra neurons. Connecting neurons from early experience instead of in utero is the way we do that. Recognizing the power of those early circuits helps us manage them.

Myelin and Change

The modern idea that we can always change our brain is an oversimplification. It's more realistic to say that we can adapt our early circuits than to believe we can uproot and replace them. We peak at age two from the myelin perspective. A toddler's brain develops so easily in response stimulation that it absorbs everything uncritically. After age two, a brain starts to rely on the circuits it has rather than changing itself in response to each new input. You keep learning and seeking novelty, of course. But instead of giving equal importance to every detail that reaches your senses, you start paying attention to variations in things you've seen and heard before. This is how we come to make sense of words and faces.

Myelin stays high until age seven, so new inputs easily build new pathways until then. A good way to test this is to lie to a six-year-old and an eight-year-old. The six-year-old will absorb what you say as the truth. The eight-year-old will check it against his existing stock of knowledge. An eight-year-old does not change his view of the world with every new input. The drop in myelin motivates a child to use the circuits he has instead of always building new ones. He adds new leaves to his neural trees, and even new branches with sustained effort, but relies on the trunks he's already built. This enables him to meet his needs in ways that worked before instead of blowing with every new wind.

What did you learn by age seven that's relevant to survival? You didn't learn to qualify for a job with benefits. You didn't learn to create an online dating profile that attracts the perfect mate to reproduce your genes. You learned to manage your sense of threat. Without conscious intent, you connected neurons each time you felt threatened and each time you enjoyed relief from threat. You learned that making noise brings relief, so you learned new ways to make noise. You learned the sounds that predict relief, so you learned to listen for those sounds. Happy and unhappy chemicals build bridges between all the neurons active at the moment they're released. These bridges help the chemicals turn on again in similar circumstances.

Any pathway that's triggered repeatedly gets myelinated. You may hear a child effortlessly command a language or a sport that you struggle with. Yet you can effortlessly command the language and physical skills you learned in your childhood. In the same way, some neurochemical responses come to you effortlessly because you myelinated them in youth. Other neurochemical responses might be a struggle for you, but you can wire them in if you invest the effort it would take to master a sport or a foreign language. Things that triggered your internal alarm bells in youth will easily trigger you later on. Things that relieved your internal alarm in youth are likely to relieve you later on.

By the time you were eight, you had a mental model of how the world works. It wasn't complete or perfect, but it guided you toward rewards and away from pain. To a child, something is good if it feels good and something is bad if it feels bad. This is not the best survival strategy in the modern world, so it's a good thing we keep building our mental model. Eventually we learn that good feelings can lead to bad outcomes and bad feelings can lead to good outcomes. Nevertheless, our foundational circuits rest on simple mammalian responses.

Of course, we can't learn everything from experience. You'd get run over by cars and expelled from playgroups if you had to learn everything the hard way. To avoid this, adults structure the rewards and pain in a child's environment. Hugs and praise and treats create good feelings in the short run for things that are good for the child's long run. Bad feelings are created in the short run to help a child learn what's bad for their well-being in the long run. One of the first things a child learns is that a bad feeling will get worse if he or she does not relieve it. Children build their operating system from pleasure and pain, not from conscious intent, so adults organize the pleasure and pain in ways that build useful circuits. Over time, we learn to interpret our internal sense of alarm and act to relieve it.

The **Human Brain** Says . . .

Children build their operating system from pleasure and pain, not from conscious intent, so adults organize the pleasure and pain in ways that build useful circuits.

The importance of our first seven years of learning is apparent when you compare it to the childhood of an animal. A mouse reaches puberty in four months, so it can be a great-grandparent at age one. A gazelle runs with the herd the day after it's born. An elephant learns to walk before its first meal because that is how it gets to the mother's milk. Animals learn to meet their needs fast because threats are urgent in the state of nature. The extended dependency of humans is unique in nature. Early learning is the foundation of our adult responses, whether we like it or not.

PUBERTY RESET

Myelin spikes again in puberty, so we build new circuits easily at that time. The ability to myelinate new learning during puberty has tremendous survival value. Animals tend to leave home before they mate, and myelin helps a brain adapt to its new environment. Leaving home prevents inbreeding and thus promotes survival, so natural selection built a brain that supports this. Conscious intent to avoid inbreeding is not required.

Humans have sought mates in other groups throughout history. When they went to new tribes, they learned new faces, new places, new survival skills, and even new languages. The neuroplasticity of adolescence made it possible. Myelin drops after puberty, and then it takes a lot of repetition or a huge neurochemical spike to fuse new circuits. That's why we're so heavily affected by our adolescent experience. Adolescent learning happens in the usual mammalian way: in response to pleasure and pain. Social rewards and social pain trigger lots of neurochemicals, so they make a big contribution to the neural network that guides our future expectations and decisions.

Anything relevant to reproduction gets an extra large response from the mammal brain. Big bursts of chemicals are triggered by the quest for mating opportunity because it's so relevant to survival.

From the pain of romantic rejection to the pleasure of social cliques, things feel urgently important in adolescence because they're important to a mammal. Bad hair or an unrequited glance can feel like a survival threat, and big circuits get built. You don't consciously care about your genes, and monkeys don't either, but "reproductive success" triggers big neurochemical spurts over small things because brains with those responses made more copies of themselves.

We know the brain is always learning from what works and, in adolescence, what works is healthy looks, social alliances, and a willingness to take risks. You may blame this on our society, but those factors have triggered our neurochemistry since the dawn of time. Anything that enhances an adolescent's appearance, social alliances, or risk tolerance triggers happy chemicals and builds circuits. And whatever threatens your appearance, social alliances, or ability to take risks brings floods of cortisol.

Whatever relieved your threatened feelings in adolescence built superhighways in your brain. Cynicism may have worked. You may have looked at the kids who had what you wanted and said, "They're all jerks." It felt good, which paved the way for you to see it that way again.

Beneath the verbal logic of adulthood lies an operating system focused on things relevant to reproductive success. No one intends to see the world through the lens of their adolescent experience, but we build our lens with the brain we've inherited.

The **Mammal Brain** Says . . .

Beneath the verbal logic of adulthood lies an operating system that is focused on things relevant to reproductive success. No one intends to see the world through the lens of their adolescent experience, but we build our lens with the brain we've inherited.

TRADITION

In the state of nature, sex leads to babies. For most of human history, people didn't decide to have children. They decided to have sex and ended up with a baby. They struggled to relieve the baby's crying, and the struggle increased as more babies arrived. Our ancestors had little free time to rewire themselves after puberty. We humans evolved to wire ourselves in youth and then get busy wiring the next generation. Now, the family-planning revolution has given us unprecedented opportunity to focus on our own rewiring if we choose. This is a new step in human experience, which helps us understand why the endeavor to change your early wiring is harder than you expect.

Mirror Neurons

Each brain has special neurons that activate when we watch someone else get a reward or avoid pain. These "mirror neurons" play a big role in social learning. Watching others triggers less electricity than experiencing something yourself, but if you watch repeatedly, it's enough to bridge your neurons. What you watch in your myelin years wires you to execute that behavior yourself. A young monkey wires itself to get rewards in ways it sees others get rewards, and to avoid pain in ways it sees others avoid pain.

Mirror neurons help us understand the many self-destructive behaviors in our world. Ordinarily, a mammal wouldn't inflict pain on itself just to enjoy the relief. That wouldn't promote survival. But if you see others engaging in a self-destructive behavior, and you get a small reward, it's easier to start. And once you start, it's easier to repeat. It feels bad. But the distraction, the social solidarity and perhaps some endorphin feel good. That wires in the expectation that it will feel good again.

SELF-DESTRUCTIVENESS AND THE QUEST FOR SAFETY

Your brain can "learn" that a cookie relieves a threatened feeling. Each time you eat a cookie in a bad moment, the circuit builds. Soon, your brain expects cookies to relieve threats. You don't think that consciously, of course. But the thought of not eating a cookie starts to feel unsafe. Eating too many also feels bad, but the bad feeling triggers a search for relief, which triggers the thought of more cookies. Similarly, a brain can "learn" to seek relief in cynicism. A person might curse "the system" when they feel threatened, perhaps mirroring others who curse "the system." With repetition, you can end up wiring yourself to curse the system whenever you feel threatened. As electricity flows through this well-developed channel, you feel like you're just seeing the obvious. The habit is self-destructive if it substitutes for action that meets your needs and avoids harm. You can end up with more cortisol, and the urge to relieve it with more cynicism.

The Apocalypse in Front of You

The animal brain focuses on threats it can see, hear, or smell, but the big human cortex can imagine abstract, intangible threats. This is why we humans are aware of our own mortality. We struggle for survival with the certain knowledge that our struggle will someday fail. We don't need to see a lion to know that something will kill us someday. We don't know what will kill us, so we're motivated to anticipate every possible threat. Each person must find a way to manage their cortisol while living with this death sentence. Belief in an afterlife is one way. Distraction is another. And some people say, "Cigarettes may kill me later, but I'll have a heart attack right now if I don't have one."

Cynicism is a popular response to this existential dilemma. Focusing on the idea that the whole world is doomed can distract you from the fact that your mortal body is doomed. On the surface, it may seem like this increases the pain. But when you believe the whole world will end when you end, it relieves the feeling that you'll miss out on something. People don't consciously think the world will die when they die. But we scan for external evidence that fits our internal sense of threat. If your brain is looking for signs of "the end," you will see a world on the brink of disaster. And it will seem obviously true.

There are other ways to manage our sense of mortality. Building something that lasts is a popular one. It could be a child, an organization, a monument, an immortal soul, or a work of art. When you focus on building something that lasts, your inner mammal has the good feeling of promoting its survival.

But this strategy leads to a new set of drawbacks. The smallest threat to your child, your organization, your monument, your immortal soul, or your work of art starts to feel like a survival threat. If your child flunks one test, or your organization's budget falls 1 percent, you may have an extreme sense of urgency. You will feel an urgent need to "do something," but there's only so much you can do. So you fall back on strategies that worked before, whether it's a pizza, a martini, or the idea that the whole world is going to hell in a handbasket.

A human brain can terrorize itself with its own abstractions, but we can also benefit from our ability to abstract. We can anticipate problems before they hurt us. We grow food before we are hungry, and we protect our babies from predators before they are eaten. But as soon as we solve one problem, we focus on the next one, so successes do not effectively relieve threatened feelings. Our innate vulnerability keeps getting our attention. It's hard for a big cortex attached to a limbic system to feel safe, which is why threat relievers are attractive.

When you tell yourself the world is in bad shape, you presume the information is coming from your higher logic. You hear intelligent people bemoan the fate of the world, so it seems intelligent to do so. You don't think of cynicism as an effort to feel safe with equipment inherited from your ancient ancestors. Fortunately, we have inherited happy chemicals as well as threat chemicals. Dopamine, oxytocin, and serotonin make us feel good, and that relieves or masks cortisol. Negativity is curiously good at stimulating happy chemicals and you'll see how in the following chapters.

Science Summary

Anything that relieves a threat feels good from your mammal brain's perspective. Once negativity relieves a sense of threat, your mammal brain seeks it and expects it to feel good.

- We have inherited a brain that focuses on threats because that promotes survival.

- Our natural threat chemical alerts us to evidence of threat so we can act to relieve it.

- Cortisol feels awful because it prompts action to escape the threatened feeling.

- Relieving a threat feels good, which wires the brain to repeat any behavior that has previously relieved a sense of threat.

- You can't always relieve a threat at its source, so it's tempting to repeat behaviors that have relieved threatening feelings in your past.

- A fight, flight, freeze, or fawn action can relieve a threat, and all of these actions can be accomplished with negativity.

- The fight response is an approach toward threat, despite the natural impulse to withdraw from threat. Negativity allows one to fight abstractly, and thus avoid injury.

- Flight can be accomplished with distraction when the threat one is fleeing from is internally created. Generalized negativity provides a distraction from more proximate threats.

- The mammal brain can sometimes escape imminent predator threat by freezing. Negativity is a way of freezing in response to immediate threat.

- Fawning is the mammalian strategy of avoiding harm by submitting to social dominance. Humans cynically submit to social dominance when it helps us avoid harm.

- We are born helpless and vulnerable and must call attention to our needs to survive. This early sense of threat is the core of our mental model of the world.

- Early neural circuits get updated in puberty, when social slights feel like survival threats.

- Myelin insulates neurons to create the superhighways of our brain. Myelin is abundant in the brain before age eight and during puberty, which is why early experience builds the pathways our brain tends to rely on.

- We know we will die someday and the world will go on without us. This colors our lens on life in a nonverbal way.

CHAPTER 3

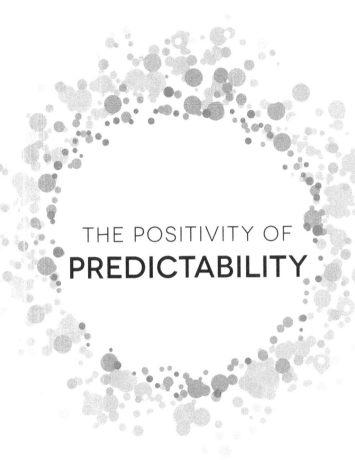

THE POSITIVITY OF
PREDICTABILITY

*The joy of dopamine is released when the
world meets or exceeds your expectations.*

Mammals survive by making predictions.

An elephant makes a prediction when it takes the first step on a 100-mile trek to a waterhole. It can die of thirst if it makes too many wrong predictions. The joy of finally meeting its need for water triggers a big surge of dopamine. That connects all the neurons active at that moment. Now the elephant is wired to start releasing dopamine, and to expect water, when it sees similar sights, sounds, and smells. This is how a thirst-stricken elephant finds a waterhole it hasn't been to for twenty years. Dopamine motivates each step of the journey, trickling at each familiar signal in anticipation of meeting a need.

Humans experience dopamine as the excitement of seeing the finish line in a marathon or taking a loaf of fresh bread out of the oven. But dopamine did not evolve for entertainment. It motivates us to take the next step when we see a way to meet our needs.

Your dopamine might start flowing when you think about your favorite restaurant. The good feeling increases when you find a parking spot near the restaurant. This is your mammalian foraging mechanism at work. In the state of nature, many nutrients are scarce, so the brain scans for them constantly to survive. Dopamine creates a good feeling when you see evidence that a need will be met.

Now, imagine your disappointment if you arrive at the restaurant and it's closed. You are relieved to see a sign that says it closes early on Tuesdays. You still miss out on the food today, but at least you can predict how to get it in the future. Predictability triggers the good feeling that your need will be met.

In this chapter, you'll learn how negativity stimulates dopamine by creating expectations you can meet. You expect bad, and you get it. That seems painful, and it is, but you also get a nice spurt of dopamine when you confirm your predictions about how the world works ("I knew it!").

DOPAMINE AND NEGATIVITY

Negativity creates predictability. When you say, "Things don't work out for people like me," you may not get what you want, but you get the good feeling of knowing how things work. The brain releases a bit of dopamine every time it confirms a prediction. A mammal meets its needs by making a prediction, taking a step, and then evaluating the results before choosing its next step. If the results are disappointing, cortisol is released, which alerts a mammal to change course. If results meet or exceed expectations, dopamine is released. Negativity helps you set expectations you can meet, so it's a reliable way to enjoy a little dopamine.

Each brain generates expectations about how to attain rewards based on its own unique experience. Unexpected rewards, like flowers from a secret admirer or a bigger raise than you anticipated, trigger extra-large dopamine thrills. Of course we can't predict unexpected rewards, and we often fail to predict the rewards we expect. But dopamine did not evolve to make you happy all the time. It evolved to store new information about rewards.

Cynicism is a way to trigger dopamine when other ways fall short. If you tell yourself, "It's all so unfair," you can always find evidence to prove it. Thus you create expectations you can meet, and it feels good.

The **Mammal Brain** Says . . .

Your dopamine flows when you anticipate meeting a need. Signs related to past rewards motivate you to keep seeking.

Dopamine makes a thirsty elephant feel good before it actually meets its need. The chemical does its job by releasing energy and a sense of excitement during the steps necessary to reach a reward. A long, thirsty trek to a waterhole feels bad, but dopamine makes each step feel good. Mammals eagerly do things that stimulate their dopamine, like foraging for food or scanning for potential mates. The big human brain relies on dopamine for the many steps involved in a complex goal. Whether you are trying to become a doctor or planning your dream vacation, your brain predicts the steps that will meet a need, and rewards you with a good feeling each time it sees that you're a step closer. It feels great to see that medical license or arrive at your fabulous travel destination, but the dopamine along the way is what makes it possible.

Dopamine promotes seeking, and seeking promotes survival. We don't always find what we seek, so we often end up with cortisol. The bad feeling motivates you to abandon a course that will not meet your needs and find a new course that triggers your dopamine. If an elephant treks for miles without seeing a familiar sign, the bad feeling grows. That motivates him to seek elsewhere, and a nice spurt of dopamine rewards him when familiar images finally appear. Meeting real needs is what counts in the state of nature, but good feelings start as soon as you expect to meet a need. Positive expectations motivate you to seek.

The world is not always predictable, of course, so our expectations get disappointed. We were not meant to surge with dopamine all the time. We were meant to keep seeking it. It's hard to do that after a few disappointments, so the spurt you get from cynicism may seem alluring. When you say, "The idiots in power will lead us to ruin," you seek evidence to "prove" this, and you feel good when you find it!

EFFORT VERSUS REWARD

A mammal has limited energy to meet its needs, so survival depends on careful decisions about where to invest its effort. If a lion ran after every gazelle it saw, it would run out of energy and starve before it caught a meal. Instead, a lion sizes up each potential target and saves its energy for one it expects to reach. The lion has a database of expectations because past successes triggered dopamine, which connected neurons. When a lion sees a gazelle that's close and weak and alone, dopamine surges and sparks the action.

Dopamine tells your brain to release the reserve tank of energy. If you did that all the time, you would run out of energy before you met your needs. Instead, your brain saves your energy until it sees evidence that rewards are likely. It defines rewards from experience, which includes the imagined experience a big cortex can trigger, such as performing in Carnegie Hall. Rewards are also defined by unmet needs. If you are dehydrated, the path to water will make you feel good, but once your water needs are met, the path to water will not turn on your dopamine. If you were starving, the promise of bitter herbs would excite you, but once your caloric needs are met, those bitter herbs don't seem rewarding. Once your physical needs are met, social needs get your mammal brain's attention. It's easy to see why so many people want to perform in Carnegie Hall. We build expectations about ways to meet social needs, and feel good when we step toward them.

Our conscious mind tends to focus on a big, concrete goal in anticipation of a big dopamine spurt. But small spurts of dopamine are needed to motivate each step. Consider all the steps involved when a monkey sees a luscious piece of fruit at the top of a tree. The first step is deciding whether the expected reward exceeds the expected effort. If she's hungry and the tree looks climbable, dopamine is released and the monkey starts planning her course of action. She scans for the best route to the treetop and the best first step. Before putting her weight on that first branch, she tests it. Dopamine is released if there's a positive prediction based on past climbing experience. Once she's safely on the first branch, she chooses and tests her next step, and the next squirt of dopamine initiates it. The path to reward is paved with many drips of dopamine.

The **Mammal Brain** Says . . .

The path to reward is paved with many drips of dopamine.

The going gets tougher as the monkey approaches the fruit. The branches are thin, the ground is far, and rival monkeys get in her way. She gets more careful, which means confirming expectations in more detail. Her dopamine surges when the fruit is just within reach. All the neurons activated by the effort get bridged to the dopamine pathway, which improves her seeking skills in the future.

Dopamine builds skills without effort or intent. Imagine your ancestors stumbling on a bountiful fishpond. They would have gotten very excited because protein is a big reward in the state of nature. Protein is critical to reproductive success, and meeting a big need triggers a big spurt of dopamine. All the sights, sounds, and smells of the moment got connected, which helped your ancestors find more fish in the future. Good feelings motivated them to seek more fishponds in the expectation of more good feelings. We don't always know why we have a good feeling about something because the pathway doesn't rely on words.

Unfortunately, good feelings can steer us wrong. Lions fail in 95 percent of their chases. Monkeys climb to treetops only to lose the fruit to a rival. Your ancestors trekked to fishponds that had already dried up. Cortisol tells a mammal to stop investing in an unrewarding path. But dopamine helps a mammal get excited about a promising new path.

Social Rewards

Your brain focuses on social needs when immediate survival needs are met. For example, who you sit with at lunch matters little if you are starving. But once your basic needs are satisfied, lunch with special company can trigger lots of dopamine. Unfortunately, social rewards can be hard to predict. That special lunch you've expected can fail to materialize. Lots of cortisol can result from seeking social rewards. You try to make good predictions, but your fellow mammal does not always reward you as expected. When life fails to fit your expectations, it can be hard to choose your next step. People often fall back on cynicism to reorient. You can tell yourself, "Nothing works out in this messed-up world," and you can always find evidence that your prediction is right.

"Not me," you may say. "I just want the facts." We don't imagine ourselves sifting the world for evidence that confirms our expectations. But that is what the brain is designed to do. In a world of sensory overload, we're designed to scan for data that fit expectations instead of wasting our limited bandwidth on random inputs.

EXPECTATIONS VERSUS REALITY

We must constantly generate expectations in order to make sense of the world. For example, when you read, you are constantly predicting what letters and meanings will come next. Dopamine squirts when the information on the page matches your expectation, and then you generate the next prediction and the next dopamine squirt. You can make sense of a typo, or a sign with letters missing, or a word written in dancing girls, even though they're not a perfect fit, because your expectations are always filling in the blanks. You do this so easily that you don't even notice unless the mismatch is so big that cortisol alerts you to reread the sentence.

In much the same way, you are always making predictions about how the world works. When a prediction is wrong, it feels like a survival threat until you correct it, so we are always looking for ways to improve our predictions about the world. Any time you can predict threats and obstacles, dopamine trickles and it feels good.

When you tell yourself, "The little guy doesn't have a chance," you have the good feeling of knowing how the world works. You have a way to make predictions that avoid disappointment. You are still "open to the facts," but your brain makes decisions about which facts matter. A hungry lion ignores the gazelle that's out of reach. A thirsty elephant ignores the path that doesn't lead to water. Your brain strives to predict the path with the best reward for effort and protection from harm.

PREDICTING SOCIAL REWARDS

A mammal must meet social needs in order to keep its genes alive. When it gets a social reward, like the attention of a powerful ally or desirable mate, happy chemicals pave a pathway that help it find more social rewards in the future. The mammal brain is always making predictions about how to meet social needs. When you get a step closer to a social reward, dopamine flows and you plot your next step. If you succeed at getting the expected job or date or smile of approval, you strengthen that dopamine circuit. But the good feeling is soon metabolized and your brain is soon looking for a way to get more. It would be nice to have a guaranteed formula for social rewards, but despite our best efforts, our social expectations are sometimes disappointed.

Sometimes, a monkey grooms another monkey and gets nothing in return. Sometimes an ape courts a mate and gets completely ignored. Cortisol prompts a mammal to try something different, but after a few disappointments it can be hard for the mammal to predict where to invest its energy. This is why we often fall back on the neural superhighways we myelinated in youth. Your electricity flows effortlessly down the pathways built by behaviors that were reliably rewarded in your past. Maybe it was scoring a touchdown, or joining friends to watch your favorite quarterback score. Of course, carrying a ball across a line does not meet real survival needs, but dopamine surges when you expect a social reward. Each brain predicts social rewards from its own life experience. Maybe you lived in a world where social rewards went to someone who cooked a big meal or solved a big equation or found a bar open after hours. There are limitless ways to get social rewards, but the ones we observe and enjoy in youth build expectations that last.

Many people get social rewards from cynicism. They see that condemning the world gets respect. They expect that good feeling when they condemn the world. Soon, the good feeling is metabolized and they condemn the world again.

WHY THE WORLD DISAPPOINTS

Your dopamine does not surge if you return to the same fishing hole every day. You'd have to find a bigger fishing hole to get it because your brain takes the rewards you have for granted. Before you blame this on "our society," consider this landmark study.

Researchers trained monkeys to do a task in exchange for spinach leaves. One day they surprised the monkeys with an unexpected reward—sweet apple juice—instead of spinach. The monkeys' dopamine skyrocketed, because sugar provides more energy for survival. Dopamine is the brain's way of saying, "This *really* meets your needs. Get more of it!" But the monkeys' dopamine fell after a few days, even though the juice kept coming. Eventually, the juice got no dopamine response at all. It was just as sweet, but it was not new information. Dopamine's job is to wire in new expectations. Once the monkeys expected the juice, it was not a new reward, so it didn't trigger dopamine.

This experiment had an exciting climax. The researchers switched back to spinach rewards instead of juice. The monkeys flew into a rage. They screeched, flailed, and threw the spinach back at the researchers. It was a huge disappointment, but the climax gave the researchers important information.

The mammal brain is always comparing rewards to expectations. A reward that exceeds expectations thrills us with dopamine. A reward that falls short alarms us with cortisol. These neurochemical ups and downs motivate a mammal to keep seeking, which promotes the survival of its unique individual essence. But the constant ups and downs leave humans feeling frustrated in otherwise comfortable lives.

The **Mammal Brain** Says . . .

The mammal brain is always comparing rewards to expectations. A reward that exceeds expectations thrills us with dopamine. A reward that falls short alarms us with cortisol. These neurochemical ups and downs motivate a mammal to keep seeking, but the ups and downs leave us feeling frustrated in otherwise comfortable lives.

It's hard to face the world with a brain that seeks dopamine. When you get what you seek, the thrill doesn't last, but losing the reward that failed to make you happy can still make you sad. You may have noticed this paradox in yourself or in others. You may have blamed society or personality without knowing that every mammal has the same response. There is no royal road to dopamine. The brain we've inherited saves the happy chemicals for new ways to meet its needs. So instead of being happy by just existing, we have to keep seeking, adjusting to disappointments, and seeking again.

Imagine winning a spelling bee in second grade, and getting a social reward that exceeds your expectations. Your dopamine soars, which wires you to think, "this really meets my needs!" The resulting neural pathway gives you a good feeling when you study spelling words because you anticipate a reward. But after you win a few more spelling bees, the same reward is no longer special. It's hard to trigger the excitement necessary to motivate all that effort. Your brain looks for new rewards and learns from observation. You see people getting bigger rewards for other accomplishments, and you build new expectations.

Rewards that are more relevant to survival trigger more dopamine. Imagine a child watching a doctor cure her mother of a serious illness. Now she gets a huge spurt of dopamine from the thought of being a doctor. A child is thousands of steps away from being a doctor, but dopamine makes those steps feel good as long as the goal appears closer with each step. There are obstacles and setbacks, but the student keeps investing effort as long as her expectations are met. When she finally cures her first patient, she may get a huge burst of dopamine, and the rewarding feeling may last for a while. But eventually, the brain habituates to the same old reward. That doctor may feel like something is missing. Dopamine is missing.

Every brain experiences that "something is missing" feeling. Becoming a rock star would only stimulate your dopamine for a short time, and then your brain would seek more. Becoming president would not make your brain happy forever. You would think about a second term, and then about your place in history. That's what it takes to get more dopamine. The mammal brain habituates to old rewards and seeks new ones.

People often learn to spark that old feeling by embracing new goals. A doctor pursues a new specialty. A rock star creates a new image. A video-game lover finds a new level and then a new game. An athlete climbs a higher peak and a gambler risks higher stakes. But this is hard to do, so the "something is missing feeling" can linger. It might convince you that something is wrong with the world if you didn't understand the mammal brain.

When you succeed at setting your sights on a new goal, you risk disappointment on your new path. And if you reach your new goal, the dopamine won't last. You habituate, move on, and risk more disappointment. So even if you are very effective at reaching goals, your attention is always focused on the obstacles in your way. Something always seems wrong, even if you're doing well. That's your survival system doing the job it evolved to do.

ADULTHOOD DISAPPOINTS

When you're young, it's easy to imagine a fabulous future. You think you'll be happy all the time when you don't have a bedtime and no one makes you take tests. Then things get harder than you expect. In puberty, you long for social rewards and get disappointed sometimes. You see others get rewards, and your brain tries to figure out what works. You build expectations. "Someday, I'll be the one who's getting it." But when you get what you seek, your brain seeks more. If you get invited to a party, you expect to get invited to another party. If you do well on a test, you expect to do well on the next test. Once you expect these rewards, it takes a bigger reward to excite you. Anything less frustrates you.

The frustrations of maturing are eerily captured by videos of young monkeys trying to crack open nuts. In the monkey world, you only get to eat nuts if you crack them open yourself. Nuts are very motivating because fat and protein are scarce in the state of nature, so they trigger lots of dopamine. But adult monkeys never provision their little ones with nuts. Children pick scraps from their mother's shells, and the reward wires them to seek more. They watch others get the reward, and mirror the behavior. But cracking nuts is not easy. It can take years to get the hang of it. A young monkey keeps trying because there are few ways to get such a dopamine rush. If a monkey gives up, it misses out on the nutrition and the strength that nuts bring, which means its genes are less likely to get passed on. We are not descended from individuals who said, "Something is wrong with these nuts." We are descended from individuals who persevered until they got the reward.

The **Mammal Brain** Says . . .

We are not descended from individuals who said, "Something is wrong with these nuts." We are descended from individuals who persevered.

During your myelin years, you saw others crack open nuts and you built expectations. Things didn't always work out as you predicted, however, because adolescent experience is never a perfect representation of how the world actually works. Alas, the pathways you myelinated are still there shaping your expectations. Whether you hoped to get a lot of nuts while others look on admiringly, or expected a world in which others get the nuts, it's easy to end up with frustration and cortisol.

Maybe you imagined a world in which things go your way, but once you cracked a few nuts, it stopped feeling like a big deal. Maybe you see others cracking bigger nuts, faster. Your cortisol flows as you think, "This is not what I expected!" Maybe your first cracking efforts failed, and you learned to give up to avoid frustration. When you think other people get all the nuts, you can easily find evidence.

Maybe you succeeded at nut cracking but smashed your fingers on a rock in the process. You learned to expect pain along with your nuts. Now you keep smashing your fingers because you know that works. You don't seek an alternative because you're wired to expect pain.

ANTICIPATING THE WORST

Imagine a monkey trying to eat lotus roots in crocodile-infested waters. He keeps enjoying a delicious meal as long as he can see that the predator is still on the other bank of the river. His dopamine spurts every time he looks up and sees the crocodile where he expects it to be. The good feeling tells him to go for it, and he meets his needs with another lotus root. If he did not see the crocodile in the expected place, his cortisol would spurt, and tell him to do something fast to make the cortisol stop.

Seeing the crocodile feels good compared to not seeing it. When a threat fits your expectations, it feels like you have it under control. You can get back to meeting your needs, and that feels good.

Negativity often gives people the feeling of having a threat under control. A cynical thought is like looking up and seeing the crocodile in the expected place. You can say, "It's all going to hell just like I figured," and then you can go back to enjoying your lotus roots.

When you were a child, you got rewards by predicting the behavior of others. You expected to have more power over rewards when you grew up, but adult life often gives us the feeling that others control the rewards. When you're disappointed, it's easy to blame others rather than your youthful expectations. It's easy to feel like others are predators, even though you don't think that consciously. You may find yourself monitoring people the way the monkey monitors the crocodile. You can end up focusing much of your attention on "the idiots who are messing things up."

Our brain is always learning from bad feelings. They teach us which danger signs to watch for in a world of information overload. A gazelle knows the difference between a lion on the prowl and a lion just passing through. Correct prediction is a life-or-death matter, yet every gazelle can do it. You have inherited a brain that's good at finding problems. If you look at a beautiful mosaic with one tile missing, your attention focuses on the missing tile. Even if thousands of tiles are perfectly placed, you notice what is wrong. You don't mean to judge, but your brain defines contrast as important information. In the state of nature, a pair of eyes in the dark or a rotten spot on a piece of meat are contrasts with urgent survival value. The human brain finds it easy to zoom in on the contrasting tile, and hard to ignore it.

Babies scan for contrast as soon as they're born, which is why they focus on people's eyes before they know what eyes do. Toddlers enjoy finding contrasts, which is why they enjoy the *Sesame Street* song

"One of These Things Is Not Like the Others." Finding the pattern in a mass of detail promotes survival and it stimulates dopamine.

Our big cortex enables us to compare and contrast complex patterns instead of just simple ones. The uniquely human part of your brain organizes and manipulates data in sophisticated ways, but it's motivated to find patterns because your inner mammal makes it feel good. The patterns you've wired in from past experience help you find similar patterns in the world around you. Your brain simply compares the neural circuits triggered by new inputs to the circuits you've already bridged. You hardly notice because you've been doing it since you were a toddler. When you encounter a threat or obstacle, you become wired to recognize that pattern in the details around you. So it's not surprising that people see a pattern of threats and obstacles in their world.

THE PROMISED LAND

This brain we've inherited keeps seeking rewards despite setbacks and frustrations. Small brains seek tangible rewards, but big brains like ours can seek abstract rewards that we have not actually experienced. For example, you can imagine the applause of an appreciative audience, the affection of a mysterious stranger, or the taste of a new dish you're inventing.

When your dopamine droops, it feels good to imagine a world that rewards you all the time. You can imagine steps you can take to create such a world, and the expectation triggers dopamine. That motivates you to repeat these thoughts, and soon your mental image of a better world becomes a big fat circuit in your brain. The world you've imagined feels more rewarding than anything you expect from the world you actually live in.

Once you wire a promised land into your brain, dopamine is triggered by every step toward it. If you surround yourself with people who share your expectations, the excitement builds. It's easy to see why people form social alliances around anticipated rewards.

People have always imagined a better world. When they were hungry, the better world had plenty of food. When people lacked romantic choice, their better world let them choose their partner. The promised land is always defined by the pain you seek to relieve. If the worst pain in your life is watching other people crack open more nuts than you, your promised land is a place where no one cracks open more nuts than you. Each step you take toward this land stimulates the nice dopamine feeling of approaching rewards.

But that good feeling comes at a price. Your real world seems shabby in contrast to the better world you've imagined. It gets shabbier if your efforts are invested in the imagined world rather than the real world. Sometimes people neglect their real needs because they expect a better world to meet their needs for them. The quest for a world without pain can end up causing pain. Instead of doing something to stop the pain, they imagine a pain-free promised land and focus on that. More pain may result. You may know people with self-destructive habits who frequently invoke a "higher cause." They plan to stop drinking/smoking/using/splurging/gaming as soon as the world smiles upon that cause, but the right time never seems to come.

Animals do not expect the world to be different from what it is. They do not expect to rid the world permanently of predators and rivals. They do not expect to banish bad feelings forever. They focus on the data reaching their senses. We humans can reconfigure old inputs into new information with the brain structure behind our forehead. Apes don't even have a forehead. Their skull slopes back just above the eyebrows and they live without imaging utopias or apocalypses. Of course there's great value in the human impulse to imagine change. But that doesn't give us a free pass to ignore reality. We cannot just live in the reality we construct in our forebrain. The job of our prefrontal cortex is to generate alternative expectations that better predict reality. That's where our power to solve problems lies.

THE CROSSROADS OF HISTORY

Animals cannot imagine their own death, but the human abstraction generator comprehends its inevitable future. As a result, our thoughts of the future are tinged with discomfort. Someday, there will be a world in which you do not exist. When you imagine this, your mammal brain feels a survival threat coming from your own cortex. It feels like an apocalypse, and your mammal brain looks for a way to relieve it. Thinking about the demise of life on Earth is curiously relieving. It feels bad, of course, but not as bad as the thought of the world merrily rolling along without you. No one thinks this consciously, but thoughts of world calamity have always come easily to people. It feels like the world will decline when you decline. It's oddly comforting to think you won't be missing out on much when you're gone. Making predictions about the future helps us feel like things are under control. It's hard to control events in your individual life, but you can get a nice feeling of control by predicting events for civilization, the planet, the galaxy, and multiple universes. The good feeling of avoiding harm expands when you feel like you are helping all life on Earth to avoid harm.

Anything that promotes survival triggers dopamine, so the thought of promoting survival on a big scale triggers big dopamine. Any way of leaving a mark on the world feels good because natural selection built a brain that rewards you with happy chemicals when you promote the survival of your unique individual essence. But when your efforts to leave your mark are threatened, it feels like a survival threat.

The **Human Brain** Says . . .

Anything that promotes survival triggers dopamine, so the thought of promoting survival on a big scale can trigger big dopamine. Any way of leaving a mark on the world feels good because natural selection built a brain that rewards you with happy chemicals when you promote the survival of your unique individual essence.

Each brain sees itself at the turning point in history. You see the future as the outgrowth of your present concerns. You see the past as the root of your present concerns. The brain interprets the world in reference to itself. When other people put themselves at the center of history, you may think it's distorted. But when you do it yourself, it just seems true.

We often hear that "the future of mankind depends on what we do now." The idea of shaping the future triggers the good feeling of living on. If you create something that survives, it eases your mammalian survival fears. But the good feeling of being at the crossroads of history comes at a price. Your personal frustrations get projected onto the grand sweep of history, and it feels like all mankind is suffering what you are suffering. It feels like you're living in a historical crisis, and all the disappointments of human history are a wave breaking on you right now.

Our pattern-seeking brain easily finds patterns in history. It's tempting to seek "the" pattern in human history because it makes life feel predictable. Finding evidence of this grand unifying pattern feels good. When other people filter their lives through a grand unifying pattern, you can easily notice. But your own pattern is invisible. It feels like you're just seeing the facts. It helps you feel safe in an uncertain world. But then you expect others to embrace your predictions and adopt your preferred course of action. It may seem like the whole world is imperiled unless it follows your plan.

If you focus your attention on the course of history, you build that circuit in your mind. The tide of history can start feeling as real as events you experience directly. A person can get so focused on the historical arena that they neglect their individual needs. They expect the tide of history to carry them. Alas, the tide of history is just an abstraction. If you don't actively take steps to meet your own needs, you can end up disappointed. Your brain will try to make sense of that disappointment, and it may turn to cynicism.

Science Summary

The brain releases the good feeling of dopamine when it predicts a reward, and negativity is one way to make rewards feel more predictable.

- A bit of dopamine is released when the brain finds evidence that confirms its predictions. Negativity helps you make predictions you can confirm, so it's a reliable way to enjoy a little dopamine.

- Meeting real needs is what counts in the state of nature, but good feelings start as soon as you **expect** to meet a need. The good feeling motivates you to seek further.

- Dopamine tells your brain to release the reserve tank of energy. If you did that all the time, you would run out of energy before you met your needs. Instead, your brain saves your energy until it sees evidence that rewards are likely.

- The brain saves its dopamine for new ways to meet your needs. It stops releasing dopamine once a reward is expected and the dopamine pathway is built. After that, it takes a new step toward rewards or a more-than-expected reward to turn it on again.

- You are always making predictions about how the world works. When your predictions are wrong, your brain tries to improve them in order to effectively meet your needs. When obstacles block your path, finding the obstacles promotes survival. Any time you can predict threats and obstacles, dopamine trickles and it feels good.

- The mammal brain is always comparing rewards to expectations. A reward that exceeds expectations thrills us with dopamine. A reward that falls short frustrates us with cortisol. These neurochemical ups and downs motivate a mammal to keep seeking, which promotes the survival of its unique individual essence.

- Finding the pattern in a mass of detail stimulates dopamine. People look for a pattern in the threats and obstacles in their world because it stimulates the good feeling that we can meet our needs. Small brains focus on patterns in lived experience, while big brains can construct new patterns that transcend lived experienced.

- When you feel like you know the pattern of history, you feel capable of preventing harm. You feel like you can protect others from harm, too. It feels good. But this good feeling requires others to embrace your predictions and adopt your preferred course of action. It may seem like the whole world is imperiled unless it follows your plan.

CHAPTER 4

THE POSITIVITY OF
SOCIAL
TRUST

*Safety in numbers feels good, but the brain
makes careful decisions about when to
release the good feeling of trust.*

The mammal brain evolved to seek safety in numbers. We humans like our independence, of course. We hate to be "one of the herd." But our mammal brain sees isolation as a survival threat. The result is a constant dilemma: a bad feeling when with a herd, and a bad feeling without one.

The chemical oxytocin causes the good feeling of safety around others. It's the feeling we call "trust." Social trust promotes survival in the state of nature, so your brain rewards you with a good feeling when you find it. Of course, trusting every critter you meet does not promote survival. The mammal brain evolved to make careful decisions about when to trust and when not to trust. It would be nice to enjoy the cozy feeling of oxytocin all the time but your brain only releases it when trusting looks safe.

In the animal world, oxytocin is stimulated by the constant physical presence of a herd or pack or troop. More of it is stimulated by extra contact with trusted individuals. Oxytocin builds neural pathways that tell a mammal who to trust in the future. The pleasure of company has a down side, alas, because conflict erupts when mammals gather. An individual might long for some distance from the group, but predators quickly kill an isolated mammal in the state of nature. Mammals evolved a brain that surges with cortisol when oxytocin dips. This motivates a mammal to seek the safety of social bonds despite the conflict.

For most of human history, people stuck with a tribe and a family for life. They spent their waking lives conforming to the expectations of their group. The thought of living without that group seemed so life-threatening that most people did what it took to sustain the bond.

They rarely "did their own thing." Today, you can survive without such bonds. You can trust "the system" to meet survival needs that a tribe or family would have met in the past. When conflict frustrates you, you can risk breaking social bonds and seeking new ones.

But social trust is harder to build than you might expect when you leave the world of your myelinated oxytocin circuits. The quest for social trust often comes with disappointments. Cynicism is a convenient way to relieve this bad feeling. It stimulates the nice "we're all in this together" feeling without the frustrations of living with an actual herd. Cynicism triggers the good feeling that all the good guys are "with you" without the complications of having them actually with you. You might like your privacy, but when you are too isolated, your mammal brain sends out threat signals. If you respond to the threatened feeling by saying, "We're all going to hell in a handbasket," it feels like everyone is in that handbasket with you.

But you pay a price for putting your trust in the cynical herd. You feel threatened whenever your herd feels threatened. And you risk being banished from the herd if you fail to conform to one of its cynical views. Banishment is a survival threat to your inner mammal. To relieve the survival threat and sustain your oxytocin, it seems necessary to run with the latest ideas of the cynical herd. You can justify your cynicism with data and "principles." It all feels true when you're surrounded by people focused on the same data and principles. No one imagines themselves being cynical just to enjoy the safety of the herd. But social trust is hard to build, so anything that triggers oxytocin is appealing.

THE MAMMALIAN NEED FOR ATTACHMENT

Reptiles only produce oxytocin during sex, which motivates them to tolerate the physical proximity of another reptile momentarily. The rest of the time, without the calming power of oxytocin, reptiles can't stand each other. They leave home the instant they're born, and if they don't leave fast enough, a parent recycles them instead of letting a predator get the energy. Most baby reptiles die before they reproduce, but a species survives because parents make babies in quantity.

Mammals can't do that. A warm-blooded baby is so hard to produce that a mamma mammal can only make a relative few in her lifetime. Her genes are annihilated if predators eat those few babies. We are not descended from individuals whose genes were annihilated. We are descended from individuals who found a way to protect their young constantly. Oxytocin stimulates that protection. Brains that produced a lot of oxytocin had higher survival rates, and natural selection built a brain that makes a lot of oxytocin.

Childbirth begins with an oxytocin surge. The fetus receives it through the blood, so we are born high on oxytocin. We are born ready to trust, with mothers primed to trust us. But the surge is soon metabolized and we have to do more to get more. Mamma mammals lick or cuddle their babies, and that stimulates this chemical in both parties.

Humans complicate the oxytocin feeling with words like "love," "compassion," and "empathy," but let's take a more practical look at it. It takes twenty-two months to gestate a baby elephant. A lion can kill it in a second. A lone elephant cannot protect a baby, but a circle of adults can. Elephants would be wiped out as a species unless they maintained groups that are ready to circle around threatened young ones. Eternal vigilance is the price of survival in the state of nature and oxytocin makes the vigilance feel good. A mamma mammal gets a good feeling when her child is close, and a baby mammal gets a good feeling when its mother is close. Each herd-mate enjoys oxytocin when they stay close.

That said, mammals can't spend all their time cuddling. A mamma mammal needs to get a huge amount of food to sustain her production of milk so that she can feed her baby. A young mammal needs to explore to develop its brain. Mammals often separate and their oxytocin falls when this happens. The bad feeling motivates them to renew contact. The reciprocal nature of attachment is the key. A baby mammal scans for its mother and the mother scans for the child, and that improves the odds of survival. A young mammal that loses its mother typically dies, despite all the heartwarming animal adoption stories. Attachment is a matter of life and death, and oxytocin makes that attachment feel good.

Oxytocin and Relaxation

You may have heard that oxytocin is the chemical that induces labor contractions and triggers the production of breast milk. Its broader role is to relax a mammal in the presence of others. Relaxing with just anyone would not promote survival so the mammal brain is particular about when it releases the oxytocin. It responds to the smells, sights, and sounds associated with past oxytocin experiences. When the trust chemical is not triggered, a mammal does not trust. It is on high alert. Oxytocin did not evolve for mammals to trust constantly, but to make fine distinctions that promote survival.

Oxytocin paves neural pathways that wire a young mammal to trust everything it experiences while its oxytocin is flowing. Thus a baby effortlessly transfers its attachment from its mother to everything encountered while it was with its mother. It feels safe away from its mother's side because its herd-mates trigger its oxytocin instead. A baby mammal cannot understand the threats that surround it, but it learns from experience. It gets a bad feeling if it wanders too far, as hunger grows and oxytocin levels fall. A mother may even bite a wandering child to build the association between isolation and pain.

The **Mammal Brain** Says . . .

Trusting just anyone does not promote survival. The mammal brain evolved to make distinctions.

Attachment to a group promotes survival because a herd is an extended predator-detection system. All those eyes and ears reduce risk sharply. This only works if a mammal runs when its group-mates run. We humans might think, "I'm not running until I see the lion for myself." But a gazelle who did that would not survive. Individuals who respected the judgment of those around them were more likely to survive. We are descended from them.

Following the crowd works for predators, too. Wolves, hyenas, and lions often hunt in groups because they get more food when they do so. Life in these groups can be frustrating because stronger members dominate food and mating opportunities, but pack-mates stimulate each other's oxytocin, too. The "bonding hormone" makes it possible for violent mammals to live together.

GREENER PASTURES

Attachments have a price. A mammal often has to choose between its social needs and its other survival needs. Imagine a hungry gazelle eyeing a delicious patch of green grass. Her dopamine is triggered and she wants to go for it. But the green patch is dangerously far from the rest of the herd. That triggers her cortisol, so she looks elsewhere. She sees a closer green patch, but it's full of bigger, stronger herd-mates. The last time she got too close to them, she got a painful kick. The thought of approaching them triggers her cortisol, so she looks elsewhere. She sees a patch of brown grass. It doesn't look very rewarding so it triggers only a bit of dopamine. Before a gazelle takes one bite, she analyzes this cost-benefit matrix. Finally she eats, but then the herd shifts and she has to analyze her choices all over again.

Difficult trade-offs between dopamine, oxytocin, and cortisol are part of a mammal's daily life. The gazelle doesn't expect a dopamine/ oxytocin high all the time. She doesn't think something is wrong with the world when she has to choose. She just scans for her best next step. The mammal brain keeps anticipating the neurochemical consequences of stepping in one direction or another.

Primates use their bigger brains to weigh even more consequences. They are more able to build new circuits, which enables them to break old attachments and form new ones. Primates can leave their troop at puberty and bond with a new troop. They can form cliques within their troop, and switch from one clique to another. They build new expectations about old troop-mates when things change. A primate builds oxytocin circuits in youth, and keeps adjusting them.

Primates have a special way to stimulate oxytocin through the activity we call "grooming." You have probably seen images of monkeys and apes picking bugs out of each other's fur. You may have thought,

"Why can't people be so nice?" We don't want our neighbors plucking bugs from our fur, but we long for the sense of mutual trust that grooming seems to embody. However, a monkey's life is fraught with difficult decisions about who to groom. Their expectations of reciprocity are sometimes disappointed, so they end up with cortisol instead of oxytocin. Fortunately, the primate brain evolved to make just such decisions.

Imagine a foraging group of female chimpanzees finding a tree bearing delicious fruit. The high-status ladies command the good spots around it. One lady doesn't fit, and she knows that her troop-mates will bite her if she intrudes on their space. She finds a less-desirable spot with less abundant fruit and more predator exposure. If she strays too far from the group, neighboring chimps may attack or kidnap her. Her cortisol surges when she reaches the limits of safety, so she returns to the comfort of oxytocin. Sometimes she goes hungry, but she survives to eat tomorrow. One day, she takes the initiative to groom the fur of the ladies that exclude her. Gradually, she may be accepted into their trust circle. Grooming the fur of troop-mates that just threatened your survival is not very rewarding, but anticipating their acceptance is rewarding. Behaviors that promote survival, no matter what they are, feel good thanks to oxytocin and dopamine.

Primates get on each other's nerves at times. When that do-something feeling is triggered, grooming gives them something to do. Stimulating oxytocin helps primates sustain the social trust they need to survive despite the inevitable friction.

TRUST AND BETRAYAL

Physical proximity builds trust because it builds oxytocin circuits. If you're physically near another mammal and they don't harm you, an expectation of trust slowly builds. (Think about college roommates bonding in this way.) But misplaced trust threatens survival. Many chimpanzees are missing fingers and toes because they let the wrong ape get too close. Relaxing when a monkey or ape gets close enough to groom your fur is a huge act of trust. Oxytocin is stimulated by touch because in the state of nature trust and touch go together.

Someone who's close to you can harm you faster than someone at a distance, which means that your quest for oxytocin could easily lead you to harm. The mammal brain evolved a way to avoid trusting those who are not trustworthy. It releases a huge surge of cortisol when trust is betrayed. The cortisol paves a new pathway that disrupts the oxytocin pathway. Thus, you remember when someone close betrays you.

Humans define betrayal in abstract ways. In the animal world, it's all concrete. For example, when baboons hear the alarm call of one of their grooming partners, they typically rush to defend them. They risk their lives defending allies and expect the same in return. If your grooming partner doesn't come to your defense when you call, the betrayal is life-threatening. Your cortisol surges, and your expectations about that individual change. You may stop risking your life for them, and start grooming new allies. Neurochemical ups and downs thus prompt behaviors that promote a baboon's survival. No abstract theories about betrayal are needed.

Mammals are always making difficult decisions about trust. A lioness may trust a lion who has eaten her cubs. A gazelle may trust the alarm calls of herd-mates who give false alarms. They are always choosing between the oxytocin of trust and the cortisol of real threats.

Imagine a classmate who makes an effort to build trust with you, and then expects to copy from you during a test. You may feel betrayed. They may feel betrayed. We build expectations about our social alliances, but others don't always meet our expectations. Each brain learns from experience. We want to trust because it feels good and helps us meet our survival needs. But we want to avoid betrayed trust because it rings our internal threat alarm. The decision to invest in a social alliance is not easy. After a few disappointments, you may say "Who can you trust these days?" It's not surprising that the cynicism habit is easy to start and hard to stop.

Temporary Trust versus Long-Term Trust

People are often surprised to find themselves trusting a stranger on a plane. Your expectations are low, so there's less risk of feeling betrayed. You can end up enjoying a nice flow of oxytocin. When the flight is over, you may not see that person again. Your brain will seek other ways to stimulate oxytocin.

Isolated moments of trust do not protect a mammal as much as reliable long-term trust. For example, sex (which I'll discuss in more detail later in this chapter) triggers a lot of oxytocin. It's a big boost of trust for a small amount of time. The oxytocin is soon metabolized and the good feeling is gone unless you trigger it again. Your brain prefers alliances that are always there. But that can burden you with conflicts and constraints, so your brain keeps looking for ways to get oxytocin without cortisol.

Concerts and spectator sports trigger oxytocin. You're surrounded by thousands of people who are there to experience the same thing as you. You trust them enough to act on your impulses during the concert or game. The bond feels real because your impulses must be withheld so much in daily life. But when the event is over, the people in the crowd will not help you survive. The nice herd feeling was just a spurt of oxytocin. Your brain would like to have that feeling all the time, but it does not like the frustrations of life in a big herd. Your inner mammal keeps trying to trigger good feelings without triggering bad feelings.

We value personal bonds because a virtual herd may not be there when you need it. Such bonds are hard to build, however, and can vanish in an instant of betrayal. So in our quest for safe ways to enjoy oxytocin, attachments to large herds of strangers can be enticing. Cynicism is one way to trigger the good feeling of safety in numbers. When you discuss "the crisis of our times," you sense that you are part of a huge social alliance, whether you conduct that discussion online, in person, or just in your mind. It's not surprising that new technologies are so quickly used in ways that build virtual herds. They help us get the oxytocin without the obligations of one-to-one trust bonds. People you know can disappoint you, but people in the handbasket always seem to be there.

Cynicism is a convenient way to gain acceptance into a huge trust network. When you curse "these terrible times" or "this terrible system," the herd can recognize you as one of them. You are not consciously seeking safety in numbers. Your verbal brain marshals strong evidence for your conclusions, which keeps your conscious mind busy while you enjoy the oxytocin.

WHO ARE YOU CALLING A HERD ANIMAL?

A mammal that sticks its head up when the rest of the herd has its head down suffers a real survival risk. Natural selection built a brain that knows when to keep its head down. You may get annoyed by herd behavior in others without recognizing that you are a mammal, too.

Once a particular herd helps you feel safe, any perceived threat to that herd feels like a threat to yourself. Even remote threats to your social alliance can trigger cortisol spikes that take you by surprise.

The **Mammal Brain** Says . . .

A mammal that sticks its head up when the rest of the herd has its head down suffers a real survival risk. Natural selection built a brain that knows when to keep its head down.

For most of human history, it was so dangerous to leave your trust circle that people stayed, despite internal conflicts that would horrify us today. For example, humans throughout history have tolerated physical violence and bodily mutilation at the hands of their group-mates because it felt much safer than the thought of leaving the group. The world is now safe enough for you to take the next bus out of town and bond elsewhere. But that doesn't always feel as good as you might expect. New oxytocin circuits don't build as easily in adulthood as they did when your myelin was high and your ability to meet your own needs was low. The new community of trust you're looking for may not appear. Even when you succeed at building new trust bonds, conflicts erupt. Your expectations get disappointed and you feel betrayed. You may think of taking the next bus that leaves the station because that is within the realm of your experience.

Mammals evolved to build social attachments in youth. In the modern world, we often break our early attachments and expect to build new ones. But new oxytocin circuits are more fragile than the ones built through extensive contact during your myelin years. We can't always replace the old herd with a new one. That's why we often end up feeling threatened like a mammal without a herd. Our verbal brain makes sense of this feeling by concluding that something is wrong with the world.

Oxytocin boosters are highly prized for this reason. Something as trivial as picking bugs out of another primate's fur feels important because oxytocin makes the world look alright. The modern world offers us a wide range of oxytocin boosters. Shared tastes in music, food, and sports are popular examples. Discussing the details of shared interests triggers a bit of oxytocin, and when it's metabolized you can discuss those details some more. Rock collectors talk to other rock collectors and geologists talk to other geologists. The social connection tells your brain that you are promoting your survival, even if no immediate survival task is on the agenda.

Discussing politics is another way to build social trust. Political topics tap into the deep mammalian urge for protection from threat. Life experience leads us to different expectations about how to avoid harm, but whatever your political views, you more easily trust those who share them. That trust helps alliances build more easily, which feels like a great survival boost. In a world of ephemeral social alliances, politics is a convenient way to stimulate oxytocin.

In the state of nature, mammals with stronger social alliances end up with more territory, more food, and more surviving offspring. In the modern world, strong social alliances promote survival in many ways. They can help you get a job or a date or bail you out of trouble. Your brain rewards you with a good feeling when you do things that strengthen social bonds because it promotes your survival.

Separating from the Herd?

Once you enjoy the good feeling of community, every little setback to your community can feel like a survival threat. The individual who does not move where the herd moves may seem like a survival threat. Sometimes that person is you. Your distancing is likely to attract predators that threaten the whole group. We mammals risk being excluded from the herd if we don't follow along. This risk is urgent from the mammal brain's perspective, so it typically does what it takes to sustain the bond. You can tell yourself you did it for your own reasons instead of recognizing your mammalian urge to sustain your oxytocin.

Herd Impulses

Animals make clear distinctions between their in-group and outsiders. The smell of a group-mate stimulates oxytocin while outsiders do not. If an animal approaches a group they do not belong to, they are likely to get attacked because the brain circuits of the other animals define the outsider as a threat. (Such defensiveness protects a group's offspring from the risk of too many animals feeding on the same turf.) An animal can get killed by its own group-mates unless it communicates its in-group status quickly. Each species has smells, markings, and noises that identify it. For example, some gazelles have a black stripe on their rump, some have a white stripe, some have two white stripes, others have one black and one white. These distictions are easily visible when a gazelle follows behind another. Human groups also develop fast ways to communicate in-group status. These communications may be serious or absurd, but the message is clear nonetheless. In the TV comedy show *Portlandia*, for example, a newcomer is told which piercings are right for Portland, and which piercings would mark her as an outsider.

Humans work hard to restrain their herd impulses even as they indulge them. People who say they love all of humanity tend to form exclusive in-groups with others who proclaim love for all humanity. Some people profess disdain for in-groups, and then they cluster with others who profess that disdain. Some people say, "We are bad," and only trust others who say, "We are bad." The urge to form circles of trust is pervasive in humans, even though it can be expressed in many different ways.

Small-brained mammals make very simple in-group/outsider distinctions. Primates complicate things with their extra neurons. A primate troop has many subgroups whose membership is fluid, and each primate continually works at building alliances that promote their own survival. As a result, old groups splinter and new groups form. A primate can find itself threatened by its own former mates, but that individual survives and perhaps thrives because it keeps grooming new allies, as well as old ones.

Humans are busy coalition-builders, too. We often feel threatened by the coalition-building of others. Even when you know they won't bite and kick you, your mammal brain perceives a risk. When another group strengthens, you risk losing resources to them. Your threat chemicals start to flow. Consciously, you know you can survive without belonging to a coalition, but you've inherited a brain that equates isolation with death.

The **Mammal Brain** Says . . .

When another group strengthens, you risk losing resources to them. Your threat chemicals start to flow. Consciously, you know you can survive without belonging to a coalition, but you've inherited a brain that equates isolation with death.

COMMON ENEMIES

Mammal groups solidify when there's a common threat. The benefits of sticking together motivate a mammal to tolerate harsh internal conflict. Lions stick together despite their fights over food because hyenas snatch the food of isolated lions. Baboons stick with troopmates who will bite them over a berry because they are vulnerable to leopards when alone. Chimpanzees stick together despite frequent in-group harassment because neighboring chimps can kill them if alone (except for fertile females, who just get adopted). Wolves and meerkats stick together though their leaders cut them off from mating opportunity, because wolves need a group to hunt successfully, and meerkats need a group to avoid predators. Female elephants stick with controlling matriarchs because they cannot protect their young alone.

The mammalian style of cooperation is encapsulated by these words from Leon Uris's 1960s novel *The Haj*: "Before I was nine, I had learned the basic canon of . . . life. It was me against my brother; me and my brother against our father; my family against my cousins and the clan; the clan against the tribe; the tribe against the world, and all of us against the infidel."

Common enemies are the glue that bonds a group of mammals. The group feels safe because life without it is unsafe. Mammals tolerate pain from their in-group because they anticipate a worse pain without the group.

A study of baby rats provides eerie evidence of this tolerance for in-group pain. The babies in the study tolerated mild electric shocks in order to stick with their mothers. The researchers presented baby rats with a warning sound before the shock. If the mother was not present, the baby easily learned to escape the shock when it heard the sound.

But when the mother was presented along with the shock, baby rats did not learn to run from the sound. Researchers confirmed that neurochemically the babies' brains blocked learning to avoid linking their mother with pain. Such an association would not promote survival.

You may know people who tolerate cruelties from those they are close to. A person might stick with a cruel ally if they expect the world to be worse without the tormentor. They ignore the harm they actually experience because they have such strong expectations of external harm.

Literature is full of stories about people who stick with their herd despite great suffering. From *Romeo and Juliet* to *Titanic*, we hear of lovers in agony because group-mates don't approve. When I hear such stories, I think, "Just move to the next village." But they never do. Leaving old bonds and trusting new bonds was rarely done for much of human history. Today, we expect our five-year-olds to build new bonds when we send them off to kindergarten. This is a relatively new development, which helps us understand why choosing a table in the cafeteria triggers so much cortisol.

Human groups have coalesced around common enemies since the beginning of time. Today, we bond around common enemies more than we realize. The sales department bonds around shared hostility toward the marketing department, and the marketing people bond around their mutual mistrust of the sales people, but they all unite against the company's competitor. Professors of classical literature bond around shared hostility toward the modern literature people, but they all join to oppose the administration. Second violins share antipathy toward first violins, and first violins share feelings about the second fiddles, but they present a united front against the woodwinds, whom they join with against the horns. Mammals bond in the face of common threats.

When cortisol spikes, common enemies are often blamed. We don't know what triggered our cortisol much of the time, and blaming an external enemy helps you relieve that do-something feeling without causing friction inside your group. When you make outsiders the source of your pain, you stimulate the pleasure of in-group trust. It's not surprising that so many groups get together and say, "Our suffering is their fault!"

Withheld Trust

If you don't embrace the shared hostilities of your group-mates, they may suddenly withhold their trust. They may even define you as the enemy. When your social allies say, "We're going to hell because of those idiots," you have to agree or you won't get to graze on their grass. If you dare to challenge the group's worldview, you may find yourself feeling the sudden terror of a gazelle abandoned on the savannah, or a baboon attacked by a coalition of troop-mates. You may find yourself deferring to the enmity that binds the group because the alternatives feel so unsafe.

When others do this, it's easy to see, but it's harder to notice in yourself. You may think you are too evolved to feel enmity. Small-brained mammals have the same common enemies for generations. They're born with circuits that help them distinguish the good guys from the bad guys in the way of their ancestors. Big-brained mammals develop new common enemies as their lives shift and change. You may hate seeing others bond around common enemies. But if you listen carefully to your interactions with those whom you trust, you will soon be able to identify the common enemy. Mammals are skilled at group action when united by a shared sense of threat.

The Confusion of Social Solidarity

Social solidarity feels so good that it leads to confusing responses. A poignant example is J.G. Ballard's experience in a Japanese concentration camp in Shanghai during World War II. Ballard reported fond memories of the concentration camp in a televised interview. His family was always together, he explained, and he was close to his neighbors. He knew the ordeal was painful to his parents and felt bad for them, but for himself, it felt good. He paints quite a different story in his novel, *Empire of the Sun*, which became the Steven Spielberg movie. His fictionalized self heroically protects friends and family from the horrors of camp life. The movie terrified me, so I was amazed to hear Ballard say he liked camp life because his father was home every day. It was a huge reminder of the power of oxytocin.

Russians who lived through Communism report similar experiences. A sense of shared fate eased the pain of political oppression and physical hardship. Social bonds thrived despite huge obstructions. You couldn't gather for meals because there wasn't enough food. You couldn't gather for conversation because secret police were everywhere. One thing you could do was tell jokes, so these small messages built big bonds. Jokes brought shared risk, which stimulated an in-group feeling. Of course, in-group conflict was high because primitive kitchens and bathrooms were shared among multiple families. But the sense of common threat transcended it. When Communism ended, the common enemy vanished. Frustrations could be openly expressed instead of having to be diverted into the subtle bonding rituals of jokes. And so people lost the chemical balm that eased the tensions of daily life. The result was so much pain that many people started to idealize the old days of their oppression. Solidarity feels so good that it can distract the mammal brain from real threats.

Cynicism is a way to surround yourself with people who share your sense of threat. Quips about the awful state of the world trigger nice trusting feelings. You feel safe with other cynics and they feel safe with you. The oxytocin is soon metabolized, but you can always trigger more with more quips about your shared suffering at the hands of "the idiots in power." Each oxytocin surge paves neural pathways that build group bonds. Renewing the sense of threat strengthens those circuits. But the brain habituates to old threats, so you need to keep enhancing the awfulness of your adversary to keep the oxytocin going. You may notice other people doing this. But when you and your in-group do it, it feels like you are just speaking truth.

You may sympathize with your adversaries' perspective sometimes, but saying that is likely to get a bad reaction from your groupmates. This loss of oxytocin makes it hard to transcend cynicism. Losing your herd feels so unsafe that running with a cynical herd seems safe by comparison. When you're not getting your oxytocin, something seems wrong with the world.

SEX AND SOLIDARITY

Sex triggers a lot of oxytocin. And since an oxytocin surge wires you to want more of what caused it, it's not surprising that mammals are so focused on sex.

In the state of nature, mating opportunities are not as abundant as you may think. In fact, mating is highly restricted in animal groups. When too many babies are born, more of them perish, so mating behaviors evolved to improve the survival prospects of the young. Mating opportunity is often linked to strength because that promotes survival. Strength often grows from social solidarity, so mating opportunity often rests on social alliances. Individuals with strong group ties tend to get more nutrition and chase off more predators. More of their offspring survive, which makes them preferred mating partners. Gaining the trust of a solid group is a popular mammalian reproductive strategy. This can be hard to do, but brains good at doing it got reproduced.

There are male and female variations on this theme, and both attest to the power of neurochemical motivators. Male chimpanzees get mating opportunity by building social bonds with other males. It gets them more meat, which attracts females and builds strength. Dominant male chimps chase rivals away from fertile females but make exceptions for their male allies. If a male chimp courts a female directly, more dominant males will interfere. Female chimps typically prefer the dominant males, so bonding with the male power structure is the way to get a female chimp's attention.

Female chimpanzees with stronger social bonds tend to have more surviving children. Lady chimps spend a lot of time foraging because they need so much food to support their almost-continual state of pregnancy and lactation. Foraging exposes the young ones to predators, so bonds with reliable babysitters promote survival. Bonding with both males and other females helps a mother chimp keep her child alive. She makes careful decisions about who to trust, however, because some chimps (even females) are aggressive with children.

Humans use social alliances to enhance their reproductive success in many different ways. You can probably think of many examples, both in your own life and throughout history.

Threats to your reproductive success (however you define it) trigger lots of cortisol. A widespread example of this is the refrain: "All the good ones are taken." Mating problems are often blamed on "our times" or "our society," despite the fact that mammals have always struggled for reproductive opportunity. Mammals have always fretted over threats to their children. Mammals have always lived with disappointments on the road to reproductive success. When you blame "our society," it builds social bonds and the oxytocin eases the pain. But you're still left with the feeling that something is wrong with the world.

EVERYBODY DOES IT

Sticking with the herd is not easy. When you see a herd moving together, you forget that each individual brain is choosing each individual step. Consider a wildebeest standing at the edge of a river while its herd is crossing. As it chooses its moment to plunge in, the threats are daunting. It will get eaten by a crocodile if it jumps in before the others, but lagging behind risks predation too. So a wildebeest tries to jump at the same time as the others, though that increases the risk of getting kicked or gored on the way down. As the wildebeest waits for the others to jump, the rest of the herd piles up behind it. Getting shoved in would be worst of all, so it hastens to take the plunge. Herd following is hard work even when it looks like the animals are just following along.

Your brain is always weighing the threats and opportunities that surround you. When you see others go in one direction, you evaluate the rewards and the threats. You ponder alternatives and weigh their rewards and threats as well. You hope for a perfect path with all rewards and no threats. When you don't see one, you may feel like something is wrong with the world.

Fortunately, there's another happy chemical to help you feel good. That chemical is serotonin, and you'll learn all about it in the next chapter.

Science Summary

Oxytocin creates the good feeling of social trust, but an oxytocin droop feels so bad that people strive to stimulate more in sometimes surprising ways.

- The mammal brain evolved to seek safety in numbers. Humans like their independence, of course. We hate to be "one of the herd." But our mammal brain sees isolation as a survival threat. The result is a constant dilemma: a bad feeling when with a herd, and a bad feeling without one.

- Oxytocin paves neural pathways that wire a young mammal to trust everything it experiences while its oxytocin is flowing. Thus a baby effortlessly transfers its attachment from its mother to everything encountered while it was with its mother. It feels safe away from its mother's side because its herd-mates trigger its oxytocin instead.

- A mammal often has to choose between its social needs and its other survival needs, so difficult trade-offs between dopamine, oxytocin, and cortisol are part of a mammal's daily life.

- Someone who's close to you can harm you faster than someone at a distance, which means that your quest for oxytocin could easily lead you to harm. The mammal brain evolved a way to avoid trusting those who are not trustworthy. It releases a huge surge of cortisol when trust is betrayed. The cortisol paves a new pathway that disrupts the oxytocin pathway. Thus, you remember when someone close betrays you.

- Mammal groups solidify when there's a common threat. The benefits of sticking together motivate a mammal to tolerate harsh internal conflict. Common enemies are the glue that bonds a group of mammals. The group feels safe because life without it is unsafe. Mammals tolerate pain from their in-group because they anticipate worse pain without the group.

- Leaving the group feels like a survival threat to the mammal brain. If you don't follow along when your group makes a move, your oxytocin droops and you start feeling threatened.

- A brain that cares about reproduction cares about social alliances. Conscious intent is not necessary. In a brain built by natural selection, social solidarity and reproductive success tend to go together. You can think of ways that the people you trust use social alliances to enhance their reproductive success. You can also think of examples among people you distrust. Throughout human history, sex and social alliances have gone together in diverse ways.

- Cynicism can stimulate oxytocin by creating the feeling that "we're all in this mess together."

- In the modern world, we often leave the trust bonds we myelinated in youth. We expect to build new trust bonds, but often find that harder than we expect. This leaves us eager for alternative oxytocin boosters such as temporary trust or virtual herds. Cynicism helps cement such bonds.

CHAPTER 5

THE POSITIVITY OF
GETTING
AHEAD

Why superiority feels satisfying.

The concept of superiority sounds awful to modern humans, but animals one-up their group-mates whenever they can. Serotonin is released when they prevail. Serotonin is not aggression but the nice, calm sense that it's safe to act on your impulses. The good feeling is quickly metabolized, however, so the mammal brain is soon looking for a way to gain another advantage. Serotonin paves a neural pathway that helps a mammal figure out how to stimulate more of the good feeling in the future. Brains that rewarded social dominance with a good feeling made more copies of themselves, so natural selection built a brain that seeks social dominance.

Humans look for ways to trigger serotonin without conflict. That's hard to do, so anything that stimulates serotonin is valued. Cynicism is a safe, convenient serotonin booster. When you put down "the fat cats," you can enjoy the feeling of being above them. Sneering at "the idiots in power" triggers a sense of social dominance. It feels good for a few moments, and then the serotonin is metabolized.

"I don't want to be superior," you may say. But when you see others put themselves ahead, it bugs you. Your mammal brain is always comparing your position to others and falling behind feels like a threat. When your serotonin droops, you feel like something is wrong with the world, even if you're sure you don't care about being one-upped. To your inner mammal, the one-down position is a survival threat. It avoids that threat as if your life depends on it because in the state of nature, it does. Seeking the one-up position promotes the survival of a mammal's genes.

"Why can't we all be equal?" you may say. Equality is an abstraction and the mammal brain doesn't do abstractions. It focuses on the concrete. If it sees a banana, it wants the banana. If it sees a bigger, stronger monkey next to the banana, it wants to avoid pain. The mammal brain is always weighing expected pain and gain. It seeks the advantage in ways that worked before.

"I don't want the banana," you may say. "I want the less fortunate to have it." Saying that gives you the one-up position in a life where you already have enough bananas. If you live among people who respect sharing, you learn to get social rewards by sharing. Insisting that you don't care about your own needs triggers a one-up feeling.

When a mammal approaches a weaker individual, it displays dominance signals understood by members of that species. The weaker individual responds with submission signals that are likewise understood. This is how social animals avoid conflict. The weaker individual protects itself from aggression by conveying its lack of competitive intent. The dominant individual's serotonin rises when it gets respect in this way. If its dominance display is not rewarded by a submission gesture, its serotonin droops and it becomes agitated.

Humans work hard to restrain the urge to dominate. That's why we feel so threatened when we think others get rewarded for dominating. We strive for fairness, but no individual is a good judge of fairness. Each brain sees it through the lens of its own neurochemistry. When you lack a sense of social importance, something seems wrong with the world. You look for ways to feel better, but it's hard to figure out what works. Sometimes, cynicism works.

We all experience social dominance with circuits built from our past. Anything that stimulated your serotonin in your youth built neural superhighways that shape your expectations about how to feel good today. You learned behaviors that got respect in the niche you lived in, and you learned to avoid behaviors that lost respect. Sometimes, you saw people seeking the dominant position and enjoying it. Sometimes you saw people losing social dominance and suffering for it. Your mirror neurons stored information about what feels good and what feels bad. You may insist that you only care about the greater good. You may take pride in your humility. But your brain wants serotonin and keeps looking for it whether you think that consciously or not. Hostility toward those you see as more dominant is one way. You can get the one-up spot in your mind every time you remind yourself that they are "jerks." But the serotonin is soon gone and you need to hate the jerks again to get more.

No matter how you stimulate your serotonin, your brain will soon habituate. An old familiar one-up position will not excite you forever. Your brain will seek bigger and better social advantages. If you rely on cynicism, you will find bigger flaws in "the jerks" in order to feel good.

The animal urge for the one-up position goes by many names in the human world, such as ego, assertiveness, competitiveness, self-confidence, status-seeking, snobbery. We seek respect, attention, importance, advantage. We call people bossy, controlling, domineering, manipulative. We want to be special. No matter what you call it, it's hard to see cute, furry creatures this way, but when we understand nature we can better understand ourselves.

I DON'T GET RESPECT

Respect is not just a verbal abstraction. In the animal world, respect brings real survival advantages. In the human world, we say everyone deserves respect. But you cannot mate with everyone. You cannot share your banana with everyone. You can't give everyone respect at the same time, and everyone is not going to respect you when you want them to. Your mammal brain will seek respect, and it will get disappointed sometimes. These disappointments feel like urgent survival threats to a brain that evolved to spread its genes.

By the time a mammal is an adult, experience has built circuits that tell it when to dominate and when to defer. Each mammal knows which group-mates to submit to, and which individuals will allow it to go ahead and meet its needs. Even if you respect everyone, you cannot give everyone your attention. Everyone cannot give you attention. Mammals compete for social rewards as well as physical rewards because serotonin makes it feel good. You may dislike people who seek social dominance and enjoy it. You may dislike your own urge for this pleasure. But you feel good when you have the one-up position and you feel bad when you lose it. The problem is not with you or the world. In fact, there isn't a problem at all once you recognize the nature of being a mammal.

You may think animals are compassionate and nurturing. You may hate the idea of animals struggling for social dominance. But research shows a clear link between status-seeking and serotonin in animals. A landmark study put a one-way mirror between an alpha monkey and his troop-mates. The alpha had much higher serotonin than the others at first. He made dominance gestures typical of his species, but his troop-mates did not respond with the expected submission gestures because the one-way mirror blocked their view of him. The alpha's serotonin fell each day of the experiment, and he got extremely agitated. He apparently needed their continual submission to keep stimulating serotonin. He needed to get respect to keep his cool.

Serotonin is a complex chemical found in reptiles, fish, mollusks, and amoeba, as well as mammals. We mammals have ten times more of it in our stomachs than in our brains. Serotonin stimulates digestion, which makes sense because social assertion is a precursor to getting food in the state of nature. Our brains evolved to seek serotonin while avoiding pain, but there is no sure-fire way to do this. You may have dreams of winning a Nobel Prize or a Grammy or just a promotion, but your best efforts may not succeed. And even when you get the social dominance you seek, it only feels good for a short time. Then your brain looks for more social dominance. You might blame "our society" for this thought habit, but mammals of every species seek status with any energy they have left after their immediate needs are met. It's equivalent to saving for a rainy day. Animals can't put money in the bank or preserve food for the future. They may starve tomorrow even if they have plenty today. So an animal invests today's extra energy in raising its status. That improves its prospects for meeting its needs in the future. When others seek status, it seems annoying. But when you do it, you just want to feel good.

The **Mammal Brain** Says . . .

I can't control what will happen tomorrow, so if I have any extra energy today, I invest it in raising my social dominance. Who knows when it may help?

Any threat to your social status feels like a survival threat to your mammal brain. When someone else gains an advantage, your mammal brain sees the disadvantage for you. You can end up feeling threatened a lot because the world is full of people gaining advantages.

A gazelle's prospects are threatened when dominant herd-mates monopolize the good grass and the good mating opportunities. But the gazelle focuses on finding more grass and more mates, and avoids conflicts it's likely to lose. Small brains survive by focusing on real needs rather than abstract scorekeeping. Big brains can keep score, making give and take possible by remembering prior encounters. Keeping score sounds harsh but it can prevent conflict by evening things out over time. We humans can tally our advantages and disadvantages for a very long time.

BUILDING SEROTONIN CIRCUITS FROM LIFE EXPERIENCE

Imagine a mother pig with eight nipples and ten babies. Each piglet engages in life-or-death competition from its moment of birth. When a little piggy gets access to a nipple, it hangs on and keeps others away. As its strength grows, it tries to seize a better nipple near the top, since the top spots provide more fat and warmth. Mother pig does not referee, so each piglet learns from experience. After a few weeks, conflict among them subsides because each piglet has wired-in expectations about which choices get rewards and which choices lead to pain. Each time a piglet wins a conflict, serotonin flows and neurons connect. That helps its serotonin turn on in similar future circumstances. A little pig feels safe to assert itself when its serotonin is flowing. But each time it loses a conflict, cortisol flows. Soon, each piglet has a neural network for seeking rewards and avoiding pain. A weak piglet learns to submit to avoid injury. A strong piglet learns to assert to get more rewards. You may think this is wrong. You may be uncomfortable with the porcine facts of life. You are lucky to live in a world where enforced rules mediate conflict. But when you see pigs—literal or figurative—get resources that you are not getting, you probably have a strong reaction. Even if you don't need the milk, you may hate to see that pig get it.

Life As a Mammal Among Mammals

You don't want to be a bully, but you don't want to be bullied either. You want to feel good but you also want to see yourself as a good person. We all build a variety of serotonin circuits and look for ways to reconcile them.

Serotonin gives you a safe feeling, not a hostile feeling. It's the mammalian sense that you have what it takes to prevail in your quest for a feeding or mating opportunity. If your judgment is accurate, asserting yourself will lead to a good feeling. But you could be wrong. You could get hurt when you assert yourself. Pain builds new connections to the circuits that control your serotonin.

Farmers and field biologists know that the weakest animals in a herd are found around the edges, where predator risk is highest. You may think the weaker ones are sacrificing themselves for the good of the herd. But that is not how the mammal brain works. Herd animals continually push toward the center. When they get too weak to prevail, they end up around the edges. If they're lucky, they have already reared their young in the center, so their genes survive after they get picked off.

You do not want to push the weak to the edges. But you don't want to be at the edges yourself either. It seems like you'll end up there if you stop pushing. You wish there weren't so many pushy beasts around. Something seems wrong with the world. When others push ahead, we don't like it. But when we push ourselves ahead, it feels like we are just doing what it takes to survive.

When others want special treatment, it may grate on you. But when you get to be special, it seems like justice. You're just catching up. Your mammal brain often holds back to avoid conflict so it seems like your moment is overdue. Social animals notice what others are getting. We've inherited a brain that tunes in to that channel.

JERKS GETTING BANANAS

The mammal brain doesn't do math. It doesn't say, "There are twelve bananas and four of us, so let's take three bananas each." It just keeps grabbing bananas while scanning for the risk of another monkey's teeth. Of course you don't do this. You restrain the impulse, so you expect others to restrain it, too. When others don't act as you expect, it triggers your cortisol. More is at stake than a banana. Your trust in your own rewards-predictor is at stake.

You have spent a lifetime building the circuits that guide you toward rewards and away from pain. When you fail and others succeed, it's hard to know what to do next. You need reliable predictions to know where to invest your effort. You don't want to be a jerk over a silly banana, but you want to know how the world works. It's hard to feel good when you conclude that the jerks get all the bananas. It's even harder to notice yourself picking and choosing the facts to support this unhappy view.

It's just a banana, but when someone else gets it, you may feel like something is wrong with the world. Your verbal brain may justify your bad feeling by saying "It's the principle of it!"

Social Comparisons and Ice Cream

Imagine standing in front of an ice cream shop all day. You could get the impression that other people constantly eat ice cream. You might think it's unfair that you gain weight from an occasional ice cream, while other people eat it "all the time" and do not gain weight. Of course, they do not eat it all the time. Your information is biased because you are collecting it by standing in front of an ice cream shop. Our social comparisons depend on our choice of facts, but we often choose wordlessly by letting electricity flow down the pathways we have. Once you wire yourself to feel wronged, you will easily find facts that fit.

SOCIAL DOMINANCE AND REPRODUCTION

Mammals are preoccupied by social comparison because it's so relevant to the survival of their genes. The more you know about the mating game in animals, the better you can understand your own sense of urgency about social dominance. There is no free love in the state of nature. Animals work hard for their reproductive opportunities and both females and males struggle to gain an advantage.

Female mammals do not want to waste their limited reproductive capacity on bad paternal genes. They don't think this consciously, but they act in ways that favor males with good genes. How they judge their males varies across species, but social status is usually involved. In small-brained species, males win status in the moment through physical combat. In big-brained primates, males can win status over time with actions that include a range of good deeds as well as physical combat. In bonobos, the ape known for its sexuality, females strive to mate with the sons of high-status females of their troop. Bonobo ladies work hard to raise their status in the female hierarchy so they can get access to the "better" males.

Mammalian groups often have "alphas" that try to dominate mating opportunity in various ways. Stronger males chase other males away from fertile females and thus father more than their share of the next generation. Stronger females have more children and manage to keep more of them alive until their genes are passed on. Animals aren't motivated by dynastic ambitions. They just do what feels good. Anything that stimulates serotonin is expected to feel good. This is separate from the dopamine "go for it" feeling, which rests on action. Serotonin creates the calm feeling that something is yours for the taking.

To get this nice feeling, a mammal compares itself to rivals and makes a decision. When it sees that it is bigger or stronger or higher ranking than its rival, the urge to assert feels safe. When it sees that it is smaller or weaker or lower ranking, the urge to assert triggers cortisol. Strong and weak mammals can live side by side because the mammal brain is skilled at making social comparisons. Humans crave the good feeling of serotonin, but we don't want a life of "might makes right" social rivalry. Fortunately, this "might makes right" mentality is now curbed by laws, rules, and social norms limiting aggression. But we still have a mammal brain that is always seeking advantage, comparing itself to others, and keeping score. It's not surprising that cynical notions get produced by such a brain.

In civilized society, you are expected to trigger your serotonin by putting yourself up without putting others down. This is hard to do in practice so your brain looks for guidance in what worked before. As far as your brain in concerned, anything that got you respect in your past seems like it should work. But the world does not always respond the way you expect, so your efforts to stimulate serotonin sometimes get disappointed.

We build expectations about how to get respect when we are young. Many of us learn to get respect by deferring to others. In the modern world, deferring actually helps you get bananas and mating opportunities. But it's not really deferring if you do it with the assumption that the other person will defer back to you. Let's say you bump into someone in a doorway. You may say, "After you," and expect them to respond, "After you." What if they just forge ahead instead? Maybe your cortisol will spurt and you will think they have wrongfully one-upped you. Every time you reach a threshold, your brain generates an expectation. People do not always fit your expectations and you can end up with a lot of cortisol.

The **Mammal Brain** Says . . .

After you. After you. After you. Why do they make me go last?

A mammal's day is full of decisions about when to assert and when to hold back. If you assert all the time, you end up with pain because you will not have the strength to win every conflict. But if you hold back all the time, you will end up with pain as you watch others get all the bananas and the reproductive success. Your only choice is to analyze every option, which is the job your brain has evolved to do.

EVERYONE IS SPECIAL

You may say you don't compare yourself to others, but when you see someone with better hair or better abs, you notice. Your brain evolved to make social comparisons. You can end up feeling bad about your hair or your abs, despite your best intentions.

In today's world, we expect ourselves to feel on top at all times without actually feeling better than anyone. This idealized state is called "pride" and "confidence." It's hard to create this illusion because our brain evolved to make concrete comparisons. Our brain notices its own weaknesses because that promotes survival in nature. You can easily end up thinking "everyone else" is enjoying serotonin all the time and you're missing out. You look for ways to stimulate serotonin, but you notice they have unpleasant side effects of one sort or another. Every time you put yourself above others, you risk being shot down. You might drive yourself to make a bigger impact on the world in one way or another but there's always a cost, and even if you succeed, the feeling doesn't last and your brain looks for more. It's easier to just ridicule the person ahead of you instead.

Cynicism is a nonviolent, non-narcotic, nonfattening way to stimulate serotonin. You can feel superior without going to the gym, studying for the bar exam, or tolerating the indignities hurled at politicians and entrepreneurs. Cynicism makes you superior instantly because "they" are "jerks."

We hate the feeling of living in a popularity contest and long for a world that doesn't feel that way. It helps to know that every monkey and ape troop has a popularity contest. In a famous chimpanzee study, animals voluntarily exchanged food for the opportunity to look at pictures of their alpha male (and fertile females).

In a baboon field study, animals were found to gaze significantly more at their alpha than at other troop-mates. If you feel like some people get more attention, you are right. If you find that frustrating, you are a mammal. You are not thinking about spreading your genes, but attention equals reproductive success in the brain that natural selection built. Losing out on attention feels like a survival threat to this brain.

The **Mammal Brain** Says . . .

If you feel like some people get more attention, you are right. If you find that frustrating, you are a mammal. You are not thinking about spreading your genes, but attention equals reproductive success in the brain that natural selection built. Losing out on attention feels like a survival threat to this brain.

Social comparison is more primal than food in the mammal world. A mammal doesn't grab food until it looks around to see who's watching, because avoiding injury promotes survival more than any one morsel. Social comparison is more primal than sex for the same reason. Your brain keeps comparing you to others and reacting, as much as you wish it wouldn't.

Conscious Choice versus Your Inner Mammal

In today's world we can choose which social comparisons we care about. You decide how much you care about your nails, your car, and your children's grades. You could just focus on your cats and ignore everything else if you want. But whatever you learned to care about, your cortisol gets triggered when somebody one-ups you. Your mammal brain keeps noticing the advantages of others and wondering what is wrong. In order to survive, it thinks you must be special, too. No one thinks this in words, but our neurochemical ups and downs make us feel it deeply.

The **Mammal Brain** Says . . .

Your mammal brain thinks you must be special to survive. No one thinks this in words, but our neurochemical ups and downs make us feel it deeply.

A young male monkey will not find a mate until he raises his status in the troop. A young female must raise her status or she will watch her babies die from one threat or another. Status in the primate world has life-or-death significance. This brain we've inherited cares intensely about status. Each of us expresses it in our own way. You may deride the status markers that others care about while feeling intensely about a different status marker. When we're frustrated by the status seeking of our fellow mammal, it helps to remember that it's driven by the energy that drives reproduction. You might blame society for this feeling of urgency if you don't know your inner mammal is causing it.

No one is special all the time. And even when you get respect, you risk losing it. Frustration and disappointment are always part of the mammalian quest for respect. In the past, people fought duels, wore corsets, and ironed their underwear in their quest to trigger serotonin. Cynicism is a less painful way to do this. You don't like to judge, but when you tell yourself, "They're all a bunch of crooks," you feel superior. Cynicism helps us feel on top in a world full of mammals who are all trying to feel on top.

You may insist that you only care about the welfare of others. But your brain responds to whatever affects you. If you constantly deny your brain, it will fight back by producing bad feelings. It will tell you that something is wrong and you will try to make sense of that message. You may conclude that everyone else is wrong for putting themselves above you. And while you are chastising everyone in your mind, you might continue to believe that you don't care about yourself but only about others.

NOW IT'S MY TURN

When your quest for serotonin is disappointed, your inner mammal thinks the guy above you is the problem. Opposing the guy above you seems like a good way to relieve that do-something feeling. The guy could be the little old lady who presides over your knitting club or the sibling who taunts you or the political leader you see on television or all of the above. Opposing someone you perceive to be above you in a social hierarchy can relieve a bad feeling. If you oppose them in your mind, you can feel better without the risks of open conflict. If the bad feeling comes back, you can oppose them in your mind again. You can end up with a mind full of opposition in your quest for the nice calm feeling of serotonin.

When you feel dominated, joining with others troubled by the same adversary feels good. Social dominance is more easily won with the support of a group. You may hate seeing other people form cliques and herds and go around acting superior. But when your social group seeks advancement, it seems only right. It's not one-upping, in your mind, but a necessary response to other people's one-upping.

A group makes it easier to believe in the superiority of your cause, and the superiority of your strength. Your group-mates reinforce the feeling that you are dominated, and your shared circuits weed out alternative views of the situation. You start expecting to take down the big kahunas someday, and it feels good today. Cynicism loves company.

Imagine you're in a knitting club run by an idiot who doesn't know what she's talking about, in your opinion, yet she's getting the respect that might well go to someone else you can think of. Some of your fellow club members agree, and you see a way to do something. You lead them to overthrow her, and you become the leader yourself. You did it for them, but it feels good. You start running things the way things should be run. But the good feeling soon fades. "It's just a knitting club," you tell yourself. You start focusing on the idiots one-upping you in other areas of your life. You find allies and decide to do something.

Opposing a hierarchy stimulates the good feeling of social dominance when you win. You may get hurt, of course. You may lose your top spot in the knitting club while your attention is elsewhere. If you can find a way to enjoy social dominance with less risk, it's attractive. Cynicism is a way to do that. When you denounce "the idiots who have ruined things for all of us," it feels like your stature rises. You may imagine yourself a cooperative person who detests conflict and only battles the strong for the sake of the weak. But it feels good.

Monkeys and apes often cooperate to overthrow their leader. But when they succeed, that cooperation dissolves in the rush to be the new big kahuna. A new hierarchy is soon established and endures until a new opposition replaces it. Human history is full of opposition movements whose cooperation disintegrates when the common adversary is toppled, and then erstwhile allies compete for dominance. We can rejoice when this happens with words instead of violence. But we don't, because social rivalry is so frustrating.

GETTING AHEAD

It's hard to imagine innocent animals striving to "get ahead." We are taught that the urge to get ahead is caused by modern civilization, and people tend to accept this without question. But conflict over social dominance has pervaded human civilization in every historical era. People have always blamed their society. Each brain sees the world through the lens of its own life experience, and so it's hard to see the mammal brain's overarching fingerprint on each society. To illuminate the pattern, following is a brief review of common behaviors caused by the mammal brain's quest for serotonin and social dominance.

Food Seeking

The quest for a "good body" is the core of modern social rivalry. Today we associate it with eating less, but in the state of nature, food was so hard to find that a "good body" was evidence of a mate's stamina and intelligence. Food is the key to strength in the animal world. A huge amount of foraging, chewing, and digesting is needed to survive in the state of nature. Bulking up was a rare achievement. We no longer bulk up to intimidate rivals, but our brains still connect food, status, and survival in many ways.

Animals usually follow the dominant alpha when they go out seeking food. Today, we choose leaders with the expectation that they will lead us to resources. Animal alphas control who eats what. In the human world, offering food is a way to get respect. This works even when food is abundant. Our seeking system evolved to find food. Today, it's so easy to find food that our foraging brain needs stimulation. The quest for the best table at a local hot spot, the best fried chicken recipe, or the best bottle of Chateau Margaux triggers the feeling of successful foraging.

Sexual Rivalry

Sex is the reward for social dominance in the animal world. Stronger animals work hard to keep rivals away from desirable mates. "Mate guarding" happens in different ways in different species. Wolves and meerkats have an alpha pair that dominates reproduction by biting and clawing all group-mates. In female-dominated species, like bonobos and hyenas, females bite and claw each other to keep the best guys for themselves. Sexual rivalry typically consumes a lot of animals' energy. For example, when female lemurs go into their synchronized period of hormonal receptivity, male lemurs fight until the last man is standing, and he becomes the proud father of the next generation. Male lemurs lose so much of their body weight in these conflicts that they are busy building back up the whole time females are pregnant and lactating. In the modern human world, sexual rivalry is deemed adolescent, but our conflicts often link back to mating opportunity in one way or another.

Doing Favors

Animals get ahead by doing favors for others. An alpha baboon risks its life to defend troop-mates who just run up a tree when a lion approaches. Chimpanzees are known to babysit, share meat, defend, and groom their social allies. A mammal does not get ahead by putting itself first all the time, but putting itself last doesn't work either. Favors are bestowed where it promotes reproductive success, though an animal is not conscious of the mechanics. The mammal brain evolved to weigh opportunities to advantage its unique individual essence.

Avoiding Conflict

A mammal weakens if it tries to dominate constantly; but if it submits constantly, it will weaken, too. A brain good at picking its battles has the best prospects. A primate gradually gains respect by avoiding conflicts except those it can win. This is what the mammal brain evolved to do.

Preparing Kids to Play the Game

A mammal's genes only survive if its children have children. Parents teach young mammals how to get respect and thus mate and keep their genes alive. Without conscious intent, young mammals learn the status-seeking game by watching their mother. They wire themselves to assert when she asserts and hold back when she holds back. Researchers also find mamma mammals intervening in conflicts on the side of their children, and those children become better status-seekers. Each young mammal learns to avoid conflicts it will lose, but also to recognize conflicts it can win.

You may wish for a world without conflict or sexual rivalry or food temptation. You can refuse to get out of bed until a world without conflict arrives. But mammalian social rivalry has been around for millions of years, so the chance of it disappearing in your lifetime is poor. You are better off celebrating your brain's capacity to cope with it.

THE ROLLER COASTER OF SOCIAL DOMINANCE

Children often imagine themselves in positions of respect, like a ballerina or a superhero. Such dreams stimulate serotonin and feel good. When you were a child, you may have won an athletic event or a talent contest or a math game. You may have stolen a cookie and gotten away with it. Whatever gave you that "I'm on top" feeling wired your brain to do more of whatever made it feel good.

But happy chemicals are quickly metabolized, so your brain kept looking for more. You realized painfully that your status as a top athlete or math whiz or cookie snatcher could be lost at any time. You didn't like the pressure to keep seeking, but it felt essential for survival.

Bad ways of seeking social dominance have existed throughout human history. Some people have dominated others in cruel ways because it felt good to them. Even people who don't see themselves as dominant have sought respect by brawling in bars, embezzling from companies, or belittling children. Cynicism looks good if you compare it to the many bad ways of seeking dominance.

Good ways to stimulate serotonin are hard to find, so imagining greatness is very appealing. You can imagine yourself an *artiste fameuse*, a rescuer, or righter of wrongs. You can imagine yourself living in a place that appreciates your greatness. Seeking dominance in this way helps us stimulate serotonin without the violent conflict of our ancestors.

Many people think the primitive world was free of social hierarchy and conflict. But interviews with preindustrial people show pervasive aggression beneath the rhetoric of equality. There's aggression among males, among females, between males and females, between adults and children, and between in-groups and out-groups. Anthropologists who document the unpleasant side of tribal life tend to be less popular than the ones who feed our longing for a happy world. But it's useful to understand the rigid controls of tribal societies. Children learn to obey and follow. You may think they're free because they swim naked and don't have to wear church clothes, but the expectations imposed on them are typically more severe than the ones you grew up with. They submit to the customs and power structure of their tribe, or else.

We mammals can get on each other's nerves. Over the centuries, we built social arrangements that manage the tension of two mammals in one space. A cocktail party full of verbal sparring is a successful arrangement because it removes violence from the quest for social position. Feelings may get hurt, but if you expect a world with no hurt feelings, your expectations are not realistic.

Many people say that money is the cause of all problems. But before there was money, hereditary hierarchies were pervasive. The chance to earn money gave people an alternative way of seeking respect. If you get upset about other people's money, the cause is not money but your inner mammal's longing for social dominance. Those who disdain money seek social dominance in other ways. Many people feel superior about their ethics and condemn others for being "unethical" or "insensitive." This feel-good strategy is easily available, and when the good feeling passes, you can find fault with the ethics of others again. You don't consider it status-seeking, but it stimulates your serotonin. Neurons connect and your brain learns to seek good feelings in this way.

No matter where you seek that one-up feeling, the world will frustrate you some of the time. Your dreams of glory may not come true. And if they do, your brain will habituate to the respect you are getting and you will need even more. When you get respect, you will worry about losing it. No matter where you are, you are a mammal. But you can use your knowledge of the mammal brain to wire yourself to feel good in the world you actually live in.

Science Summary

Animals create status without formal structures or conscious intent. It emerges organically from individual efforts to stimulate serotonin. In this chapter, you've learned:

- Each mammalian species has its own variation of social hierarchy, emerging from the survival constraints of its ecological niche. Female mammals seek social dominance in ways that bring better nutrition, paternal genes, and protection for children. Male mammals seek social dominance in ways that bring access to fertile females and block other males' access.

- The mammal brain constantly monitors who is in the dominant position and who is in the subordinate position. Mammals don't seek dominance with aggression when there's a high risk of pain. Sometimes, they dominate by expecting others to defer.

- Brains that cared about status made more copies of themselves, and a status-seeking brain was naturally selected. You don't think this way in words, but your brain craves the good feeling of serotonin. It's released when you get respect, and it paves neural pathways that tell you how to get more.

- Serotonin is a safe feeling, not a hostile feeling. It's the mammalian sense that you have what it takes to get the resource you seek in a social context.

- Any threat to your social position feels like a survival threat to your mammal brain. The cortisol alerts your big cortex to find evidence about the threat and it paves a neural pathway that turns on more cortisol in similar situations.

Thus the brain wires itself to feel threatened by social rivals without conscious intent.

- The expectations created by old neural pathways are never a perfect predictor of the social world. Sometimes we are disappointed and end up with cortisol. Sometimes we are surprised by a nice extra serotonin boost. These chemicals build new pathways that adjust our expectations. Each brain keeps seeking respect with the pathways it has.

- Any serotonin you manage to stimulate is soon metabolized and you have to do more to get more. This motivated our ancestors to keep striving in the face of severe physical and social threats. The good feeling of serotonin did not evolve to flow constantly for no reason. It evolved to reward you with a good feeling when you find a safe way to assert yourself.

CHAPTER 6

BUILD A
PARE HABIT

*Use Personal Agency and Realistic
Expectations to build a positive life.*

Are you tired of being cynical? Ready to enjoy your own power, today, without waiting for the world to change? You can see good in the world by going beyond the information you're wired to look for. With the system explained in this chapter, you will learn to feel good in the world as it is instead of expecting an imagined world to make you feel good.

As we discussed, negativity is natural because disappointment feels like a survival threat to this brain you've inherited. Cynicism helps relieve a sense of threat, but it comes at a price. It makes you powerless, because you focus on things you can't control instead of things you can control. Cynicism focuses your attention on old expectations, which makes new threats and rewards hard to see. Negativity is a bad habit that persists because our brains tend to rely on the circuits we built long ago.

New circuits will build if you give your brain a new stream of inputs. This is hard to do, which is why people tend not to rewire themselves unless their inputs are altered by some outside force. Now that you know how your brain works, it will be easier for you to rewire your brain. But disabling your old circuits tends to trigger a sense of alarm. Your brain equates old habits with survival, so ignoring them feels like a survival threat. Upgrading your neural operating system is harder than upgrading your computer's operating system because your brain must always be on so you can never hit "restart." When you try to stop an old habit, it feels like you are losing access to your hard drive with its lifetime stock of messages and images that remind you of who you are. But if you accept the temporary uncertainty, you will soon enjoy new ways of connecting up your experience.

Persevere and you will literally forget to be cynical, because electricity will light up a new positivity circuit. What is a positivity circuit? In this chapter you'll learn about two thought habits that transcend our natural negativity: Personal Agency and Realistic Expectations, or PARE. Personal Agency is the awareness that your efforts can meet your survival needs. Realistic Expectations is the knowledge that your neurochemical ups and downs come from a quirky mammal brain. With Personal Agency and Realistic Expectations, you focus on your next step, and you enjoy taking it. PARE your attention and you are not distracted by the world's flaws.

You have power over your own circuits. Being your own personal agent feels better than lamenting the world's failure to meet your needs, and realistic expectations feel better than equating frustration with crisis. If you PARE, you will REAP, because **R**ealistic **E**xpectations help you **A**ct **P**ersonally. Anyone can transcend their natural negativity by building PARE circuits. So let's take a look at how to do it.

THE POSITIVITY HABIT

Here is a simple way to feed your brain a new stream of inputs. Three times a day, stop and think of something good. Spend one minute each time scanning for the positive aspects of situations that are currently on your mind. Do this for six weeks and your brain will be trained to look for the good in the world. Define "good" however you want. For best results, do not focus on puppies, rainbows, and butterflies. Look for good things relevant to your present reality. Here are some examples from my own positivity minutes. You can see that I'm actively constructing positives instead of passively waiting for good things to come my way.

- When someone is on my nerves, I think about the personal power I have that is not controlled by that person.
- When a tragic event gets my attention, I think about the improved responses to tragic events that were not available for tragedies throughout history.
- When I feel underappreciated, I think of how this frees me to develop my own instincts instead of being tempted to do the popular thing to sustain attention.
- When I feel conflicted about food, I think about the yummy foods I will choose when I am actually hungry, and how lucky I am to be able to choose these foods.
- When I feel separate from the herd, I remind myself that my inner mammal has many different, often-conflicting impulses, and I am lucky to be able to choose my response to each impulse in a way that enhances my long-run well-being.

This exercise may feel awkward and false at first. You may think the good things you come up with are trivial. Your old circuits might tell you that these trivialities do not make up for the horrible state of the world. But in six weeks, your positive tidbits will feel as real as the negativity so widely expressed around you.

It's important to realize that this positivity habit is not . . .

- **A Gratitude Exercise:** Gratitude puts you in the role of a passive receiver. You can find good in what you create as well as what you receive. You can be pleased with yourself as well as others. If being pleased seems weak or foolish, remember that you have the rest of the day to critique things.
- **A Relaxation Exercise:** You do not need to relax while you're doing it. Don't expect joy in these moments, nor should you judge

yourself for lacking it. Just keep finding good and your new expectations will affect your neurochemistry.

This practice trains your brain to scan for good as naturally as you now scan for bad. Your automatic pilot will change if you do something different three times a day for six weeks without fail. If you miss a day, start over at the beginning until you're able to make it through six weeks straight. If you have trouble focusing on yourself, start with things that are good for others. But be honest about the benefit to you. If you only accept good for others, you may end up resentful, self-pitying, and cynical. You may think good things only happen to others, but that's just a pathway in your brain and you will build a new pathway. Cynicism may creep into your positive thoughts. When you find good news you may think "How long will that last?" But your commitment to meeting your daily quota will keep you seeking good, and in six weeks it will be a habit. You might even surprise yourself by responding to good news with: "Maybe there's more good where that came from."

"This is not objective," you may say. But in six weeks, you will realize that your negativity was not objective either. It was just a habit. Your thought habits feel true because they sail along smooth pathways in your brain. But the boulevards of your mind were not built by objectivity. They were built by chance experiences in youth. You can build new boulevards even though it feels "not objective."

The **Human Brain** Says . . .

You may think good things only happen to others. That's just a pathway in your brain and you will build a new pathway.

"How can anyone find three good things a day in such a bad world?" you may ask. It takes courage. You risk disappointment when you look for good. This is because your brain compares what you find to how it woulda/coulda/shoulda been. Your good things seem flimsy compared to your aspirations. You may even feel out of step with others when you focus on good, and fear losing their respect or trust. But anyone can end up with three positive thoughts a day. Here's how it worked for someone we'll call "Pat."

Positivity Habit in Action

Pat chose to be grateful for breakfast on the first morning of positivity practice, since this came effortlessly to mind. But Pat immediately started thinking about problems with the food: It might be poisoned with additives, and farmed unsustainably, and not a smart choice compared to a kale smoothie. Pat was in a rush to get this over with and get to work, so the idea of being glad to have a job bubbled up. But Pat's job seemed so crappy that not having a job sounded better at that moment. Then Pat started worrying about losing the awful job in this crazy economy. While rushing to work, Pat catches a bit of news, and it's all bad. Pat arrives at the office desk feeling more convinced than ever that the world is going to hell in a handbasket and there's no way to climb out. With such a busy day coming up, Pat decides that today is not a good day to start a positivity practice. Tomorrow is a better day to get serious about this, and Pat pulls out a journal to be ready to write it all down.

DAY ONE

Showering gets me thinking about the clean, hot water I get every day. I feel bad about the people who don't have this water. Maybe our water will run out. Maybe deadly bacteria will grow in it. Anyway, I have it now because systems were created and they are working. In the past, people took great pains to get water, but I am getting this water effortlessly because a system is working. I guess that's good.

Lunch time. Crazy busy. Stop to enjoy a deep breath. Gets me thinking about friend with lung cancer. Maybe I should go for a full-body cancer screening? I need to think of something good, and it has to be now because I have a lunch date. The thought of a full-body scan makes me think of all the body parts that have to work to survive. A lot can go wrong, but right now I'm okay and that means a lot of parts are actually working. That's something good!

In bed, I think of how little I got done today. I think of the committee that sneered at my work. I think of the party I didn't get invited to. Bad thoughts come faster when I relax. How can I come up with another positive thought now? Remembering that awful committee meeting reminds me of the person who smiled at me when the rest of them were complaining. I smiled back because she got it. That felt good. Being understood by one person for one moment feels good. Why can't I be understood all the time? Why are people so . . . if I go there, I'll never get to sleep. That exchange of smiles was good. It was #3.

DAY TWO

I can't use the water thing again. What can I come up with when nothing great happened yesterday and today is going to be hard? While dressing, I hear news that the stock market is up. Not up enough for me to retire. I might hate being retired. What if they forced me to retire? Suddenly I notice my cascade of bad thoughts in response to good news. I'm pleased with myself for noticing. I count it as #1.

Lunch is over. Nothing good has happened yet. I hate the pressure of finding something good. News about a war on my screen. Starving children. Food aid stolen by armed gangs. I wish the idiots in power would do something. Not sure what. Don't want them to add to the violence. If I were in charge . . . I'm not sure what would work. People have raided other people's food all through human history. Now there is help. Food donations get shipped in from far away and people risk their lives to distribute it and to report on the armed gangs. A lot of steps have been taken already and more steps will follow. These crises have subsided in other places so this one will probably subside. The suffering until then makes me mad. I'm not sure who I'm mad at. I guess it's my way to feel like I'm doing something when I don't know what else to do. I guess I can be mad and at the same time recognize that a lot of good is being done.

Invited for drinks after work. Don't feel like going. Would rather finish work. Amazed that I'd actually prefer working to that happy hour right now. It's a good thing I like what I'm doing and that I got invited. That counts as #3 and #4!

DAY THREE

I hear a report on the economy while getting ready for work. I start worrying. I see how I worry over the ups as well as the downs. It's an emotional roller coaster that I'd rather not be on. I shut off the news. At first, I worry about missing something. Then I realize that stepping off the roller coaster is good. #1.

Get a message from a friend canceling plans for the weekend. Again. Not even a sincere explanation. That friendship seems like a lost cause. Feel awful. Can't come up with anything good after this. Still discouraged about it while making dinner. Made a fabulous sauce. A good sauce doesn't make up for losing a friend. I don't know how to fix that, but I didn't know how I would make this sauce a few minutes ago. I created it without a recipe so I guess I will create a new friendship without a recipe. There's #2.

Another message from a friend who needs help on a project. I start researching, and by the time I finish it's too late to watch the movie I'd planned. But helping a friend at a moment's notice is a good thing, I realize. And while doing the research, I stumbled on a solar-powered water-purification technology that I feel really good about. A double-header! I go to bed happy.

DAY FOUR

My first thought this morning was "I must find my something good." Amazing! I worry about whether I'm biased. But then I realize that *not* looking for good is as much of a bias as looking for it. Am thrilled that this habit has already taken root . . . so thrilled that I'm sure something great will happen today. Maybe I'll get a promotion and my YouTube will go viral and I'll get invited to the Cannes Film Festival and then who knows what will happen! I'm open for something big.

BACK TO DAY ONE
Oh no! I forgot to do my positivity practice for the past few days. How did I let that happen? I think I set the bar so high that nothing seemed good enough. Now I get it. I don't need to go to Cannes to find good around me. I'll definitely keep it up this time. And I will count this moment of confidence as today's #1.

If this book were a work of fiction, Pat would now be struck by a heart attack or the plague or a devastating infidelity. And then heartwarming new love and a big promotion would follow. Big events get our attention. But our responses to big events depend on the circuits we have. Negative circuits can put the worst face on everything, so you may as well be ready with some positive circuits.

PERSONAL AGENCY

Consider this scenario: If you were a big star in the entertainment world, you would have a big agent from a big agency who got you big contracts. You would build big expectations, and sometimes get disappointed. Other times you would get the big gig, but feel disappointed when the reward felt less than the pain. You would worry about losing it all when you saw new competitors emerge. New agents would court you and you might decide to switch. But your frustrations would continue no matter who your agent is.

You are ultimately your own agent. You make the hard calls and you live with the consequences. Instead of expecting smooth sailing and getting frustrated, you are better off trusting your own ability to navigate. That's hard. When things don't go your way, it's natural to feel uncertain about your next step. It's natural to focus on what's wrong and take good things for granted. But if you enjoy being your own agent, you can feel good even in choppy seas.

The **Human Brain** Says . . .

You are your own agent. You make the hard calls and you live with the consequences.

It's harder to trust your personal navigator after a few disappointments. Sometimes you feel unlucky in love on the same day as a financial setback. It's easy to start expecting disappointment and looking for others to blame. But you can train your brain to expect rewards in the long run, even if they are not visible in the short run.

Our efforts have long-run effects that we can't always see. It's natural to be discouraged when your efforts have no immediate visible results. But most human good has come from efforts that did not get immediate visible results. There are many examples of this.

Innovation

Our quality of life rests on inventions made by people who were often disappointed during their lives. When we study historical figures, we presume they were celebrated when alive. But in many cases, their innovations were ignored or attacked at first. And even when an innovator was appreciated, they often expected more of themselves and others and ended up disappointed. But they kept taking steps anyway. If humans only did things that got short-run rewards, we would have worms in our intestines and war with our neighbors and die by age thirty. Instead, we have comfortable lives because people who came before us went beyond disappointment.

Good ideas often get a bad reaction in the short run. You can say it's unfair. You can go on strike until you get what you think is your due. Or you can keep planting seeds and trust that they will bear fruit at a time you cannot predict.

Parenting

Parents rarely get the short-term response that they hope for from their kids. You may not live long enough to see your kids applaud your wisdom. But children are strongly inclined to mirror the behaviors they see around them. So instead of worrying about having too little influence on your kids, you might ponder the risks of having too much. Your bad habits will get reproduced if you forget that young mirror neurons are watching. Stay conscious of the mammal brain and you will make sure to model the behavior you hope your kids will absorb. They may not embrace your good habits in the short run. But you can expect them to live it in the long run.

Kids tend to mirror their parents in non-obvious ways because each generation focuses on its own survival challenges. We mammals are meant to wire ourselves for the environment we're born into rather than the environment of our ancestors. Your parents adapted to the world of their adolescence, which probably frustrated their parents. You cannot see the world through the lens of a child born today. Your children's early experiences inevitably differed from yours. But you are a big chunk of the early experience of the children around you. If you model good habits, you will be pleased with the long run reward. As a parent you can invest your effort where it does the most good: setting the example you hope will get myelinated.

Career

When I was a teenager, I had no connections and I couldn't get a summer job. I'd roam around asking for work and never got any. Those efforts were rewarded in a way I never expected at the time. They wired in the valuable skill of looking for work. In my twenties, I sent out lots of resumes and got lots of replies stating that my resume was put on file. You may be as shocked as I was that the phone rang three times when a job opened up and my resume was pulled out of a file. I got three good jobs that I would not have gotten if I had said, "There are no files" and "There are no jobs."

The Benefits of Personal Agency

I am not saying you should flood the world with resumes, or enjoy your children's indifference, or become an inventor. But you *should* focus on your next step, even if your last step didn't get the result you hoped for. Of course it feels better when the world rewards your efforts immediately. But if you limit yourself to such rewards, you're limiting yourself to things that appeal to animals. Instead, you can use your extra neurons to imagine outcomes that are not yet tangible, and keep stepping toward them.

When the world fails to appreciate your efforts, it may seem realistic to give up. "Why bother in such a messed up world?" people ask. But when you don't try, you get nothing. You can say, "See, I knew I would get nothing." And that will be true in your small slice of reality. The long-run results of your efforts are unknowable, so they don't feel rewarding. You can give yourself an immediate reward by enjoying the act of choosing your steps. If you insist on predictable results, you will end up cynical. But you can find the good in your own unpredictable steps.

The **Human Brain** Says . . .

You get a reward now if you enjoy the act of choosing your steps. Use your extra neurons to imagine outcomes that are not yet tangible, and keep stepping toward them.

It's nice to "have an impact," of course. But if you feel bad whenever you don't have one, you can end up feeling bad a lot. Enjoy being your own agent instead. You can set realistic goals and feel good about meeting them instead of always judging yourself against the mammalian urge for more. Reality matters, but you get to define your real needs.

Independence versus Oppositionalism

Personal Agency begins with a focus on your needs. Many people neglect their own needs and focus on the needs of others. This is often the fast track to cynicism. You may be well-intentioned, but your focus on others does not obligate them to focus on you. If you expect them to do this, your expectations are not realistic. Being your own agent is realistic.

You must meet your own physical survival needs before you can focus on other rewards. If you don't, your threat chemicals will keep surging. As your own agent, you decide how to divide your effort between your physical survival and the survival of your unique individual essence. But you cannot expect others to meet your needs because they are their own agent. It's natural for people to help each other, but "help" does not mean being someone else's agent or expecting them to be yours. You can respect other people's focus on their needs as you focus on yours. You live with the consequences of your choices and they live with theirs.

Personal Agency is creative, not combative. It puts your focus on building something rather than tearing something down. You don't need to fight the world for your steps to be valuable. Your old circuits may focus on opposing the world, but you can build new circuits that focus on what you are building. Getting mad often works when you're young. When it gets rewards, it builds circuits that make it easier for you to get mad. Opposing others can feel like strength, and your brain can get into the habit of opposing things. But the good feeling passes, and more opposition may not get you the rewards you seek.

Oppositionalism restricts you to the "anti" position whether it's good for you or not. If you believe you must get mad for your efforts to matter, your energy gets invested in being mad. If you believe you must build, you focus on building.

The **Human Brain** Says . . .

Personal Agency is creative, not combative. It puts your focus on building something rather than tearing something down.

Your personal agent stays focused on your next step even when the world disappoints. You can't always predict what will work, but you can always take another step. You are free to leave the prison of short-run expectations and step in another direction. It may or may not get you the rewards you seek. You may or may not get respect from friends and family, who are, alas, their own agents. The world may not meet your needs, but you might find a way to meet them if you take another step.

REALISTIC EXPECTATIONS

An elephant I know taught me the value of Realistic Expectations. He was given a birthday cake for his sixteenth birthday by well-meaning zookeepers who wanted to celebrate this huge milestone in a male elephant's life. He gulped down that sheet cake in seconds. For an animal that lives on tree branches in the wild, this was more calories than he would get from days of chewing. His brain responded with a surge of dopamine that said, "Wow! This really meets my needs! Get more!" For a long time to come, his brain will seek that burst of pleasure because dopamine connects neurons that create expectations. The elephant's brain will keep scanning for sheet cake and will keep getting disappointed.

It's natural for your brain to seek more of whatever felt good before. While you're enjoying cake, it's natural for your inner mammal to say, "This is what life can be like!" But if you constantly compare what's on your plate to such peak moments, you will spend most of your life disappointed.

A peak social experience has as much concentrated goodness as a sheet cake, and it gives you the feeling that all is right with the world. But if you expect that feeling every moment, something seems wrong with the world. When you get respect, it feels like this is the way things should be. But if you expect approval and admiration in every moment, you will end up feeling like the world is disrespecting you. Do you see how this works? When you seek cake and get it, your world feels like it's under control. It would be nice to have that feeling all the time, but that's not realistic, and if you expect it you will end up feeling like the world is out of control.

We all have peak moments when we surge with happy chemicals. We have triumphs in mating, nurturing children, reaching goals, and building social trust. Happy chemicals spurt, but it doesn't last. If you expect peak feelings all the time, you will feel like something is wrong a lot of the time. It's more realistic to expect peak feelings to come and go. We still need to seek them because it guides us to meeting our needs. But we can know that, while we're seeking them, they're fleeting. We can stop thinking something is wrong when we're not having them. That is realistic.

The **Human Brain** Says . . .

If you expect peak feelings all the time, you will feel like something is wrong a lot of the time. It's more realistic to expect peak feelings to come and go. We still need to seek them because it guides us to meeting our needs. But we can know that, while we're seeking them, they're fleeting.

Setting realistic expectations is harder to do than it sounds, because the moment a peak feeling ends, all the threats of life rush back into your awareness. You can end up with an overwhelming sense of threat, and the feeling that you must have another peak moment right away in order to be safe. It's not easy to manage this neurochemical generator we've inherited, but understanding your inner mammal can help you avoid the pitfalls of disappointment, unrealistic expectations, and cynicism.

Your Big Cortex

Your mammalian responses do not always provide you with a good guide to reality, but you cannot simply ignore your brain chemicals either. Your cortisol alarm will blare if you do. The mammal brain evolved to get your attention and it will make the alarm louder and louder if it thinks you are not meeting a survival need. You can, however, use your big cortex to lead your mammal brain to more realistic expectations.

The human cortex can create a reality that goes beyond the facts reaching your senses. It can tell you that gorging on cake every day is not realistic. It can tell you that cake is bad for survival even when it feels good. Your cortex can even recognize that an endless stream of cake would not trigger an endless stream of dopamine. If you got birthday cake every day, the thrill would fall quickly until there'd be no thrill at all—only a terrible disappointment if you lost it.

When your mammal brain has learned to expect cake, your cortex can build a new and different expectation. It's not easy for your cortex to build a new circuit without a happy-chemical surge to pave the way, but repetition can make that new circuit strong enough to compete with your old circuit. Your verbal brain can remind your inner mammal that a threat is not real, but it has to do this reminding over and over. This doesn't mean you should ignore your inner mammal, because the cortex has limitations, too.

The cortex seeks patterns, and that's all it does. It doesn't have any neurochemistry of its own. A bigger cortex can recombine old patterns and discover new patterns, but it does not feel that a pattern is good for you or bad. It just reports the information to the mammal brain. We have these two brain systems because we need both. Your personal agent uses both together to choose your best step.

Focus Your Cortex on Realistic Expectations

You can focus the pattern-seeking power of your cortex wherever you choose. When you focus it on the external world, you can miss internal information. But if you only focus inside, you miss information aspects of the world around you. We need both sources to build realistic expectations. Your personal agent is always choosing where to focus your attention, and wherever you choose is the reality you know.

If you decide not to focus on cake, you have to choose another focus. The impulse to focus on threats does not serve you, so it takes some effort to find an alternative. Your brain needs something to look for because it can't look for nothing. You need a positive focus or you will end up with a negative focus.

Here's a personal example of adjusting expectations. Sometimes, I go to my computer and find an appreciative e-mail from a reader. That feels as good to me as birthday cake feels good to an elephant. The next time I go to my computer, my brain naturally expects a fabulous treat. I can end up with a lot of disappointment if I let my electricity flow there. I must actively build an alternative expectation that's more realistic. So whenever I go to my computer, I remind myself that I like the work I am doing, and that it will bring rewards that I may not see in the short run. Now my brain has an alternative to feeling that something is wrong when there's no cake.

We all want respect and appreciation from others because a mammal's survival depends on it. Social needs are not satisfied as simply as physical needs. When you need water, you're satisfied as soon as you get it. But when you get social support, your inner mammal is eager for more. In the state of nature, social disappointments are realistic information about how you are spreading your genes. But in your present reality, social disappointments are not survival threats. You have to remind yourself of that over and over.

Occasionally, I receive a note that shows a deep understanding of something I wrote. My happy chemicals surge when I am understood, even though it's just dots on a screen. Being understood is a powerful thing. Our brains link being understood with survival from the earliest moments of life. When you were born, your distress was relieved when others understood your needs. You tried to communicate, and learned that being understood gets rewards. But this good feeling is not a complete survival guide in adulthood because we are often misunderstood by the people around us. If I invested all my energy seeking understanding from others, I might neglect needs that I could meet for myself. When we are not understood, we can learn from the bad feeling, but if we see it as a survival threat, we will live in a threatening world indeed. We are better off building realistic expectations about our mammalian neurochemicals.

We are always navigating between high expectations and low expectations. Aiming high can bring short-run disappointment. Aiming low can leave you frustrated in the long run. No path is disappointment-free, but you can get more of what you seek by continually adjusting your expectations to new experiences. It's hard to do that because expectations do not announce themselves in words. But when you focus on them, your power over them builds.

Unrealistic expectations about rules and laws are widespread. You may like a rule when it's applied to others but not when applied to you. You may get frustrated when a rule constrains you and ignore all the times it benefits you. For example, parking rules are frustrating when you can't find a spot. Parking rules benefit you by motivating other people to leave their spots. But you don't thank the rules when you succeed at finding a parking spot. You see, we tend to overlook the good done by rules, and focus on the pain. But when you do that you are training your brain to see a bad system and a bad world even as that system promotes your survival. If you focus on how you benefit from the system instead, your brain learns to notice the good that's around you. Your personal agent can build that feel-good circuit with intention and repetition.

The **Human Brain** Says . . .

You are training your brain to see a bad system and a bad world even as that system promotes your survival. If you focus on how you benefit from the system instead, your brain learns to notice the good that's around you. Your personal agent can build that feel-good circuit with intention and repetition.

People often end up with a bad feeling because the mammal brain focuses on what it lacks. It compares itself to others and "keeps score." A disappointed urge to get ahead can feel like a survival threat when you have no bigger threats around you. With a brain like this, it's not realistic to expect happy chemicals all the time. It's realistic to use your power to build new roads through your jungle of neurons.

THE FIRST STEP, AND THE NEXT STEP AFTER THAT

Start your PARE habit today! Do not wait until you feel like things are looking up. Do not wait until your friends and family think it's a good idea. Do not wait until you have a clear picture of where this is heading. Just take the first step.

A mountain goat thrives because it focuses on its footing, not on the ominousness of the mountain. A monkey thrives by focusing on the next branch instead of looking down. A gazelle thrives by focusing on individual lions rather than opining about lions in general. You can thrive by focusing on the path in front of you. You get to choose that path. Your steps will be steady if you focus on the bumps just ahead instead of thinking about all bumps on all paths. You can enjoy the act of choosing your steps, even as you travel a bumpy road.

China's modernizing leader, Deng Xiaoping, spoke of "crossing the river by feeling the stones." Your next stone may be wobbly and the stones after that are unknown, but you can get where you're going anyway. You may expect firm stones to be installed, pretested, and fully documented by others before you cross. You may condemn others when these expectations are disappointed. But it's good to remember your power to move forward by mastering the stones that exist one at a time.

You may fall and land in the mud. While you're there, you'll meet people who are stuck in the mud. Your brain naturally observes and learns from them. They may tell you it's impossible to get out. If you mirror them, you can become an expert on the impossibility of getting out of the mud. You may long to escape from the wet and the cold, but you also feel some attachment to your mud-mates. You might start expecting to stay in the mud. Fortunately, you can PARE this situation with Personal Agency and Realistic Expectations.

PARE and You Will REAP

Realistic **E**xpectations lead to **A**cting **P**ersonally. With realistic expectations about being a mammal among mammals, you take a step toward meeting your needs instead of expecting the world to take the step for you. You may not get what you seek, but the first step triggers your dopamine, which leads to the next step. Acting personally frees you from the expectation that you are a victim of circumstances. You don't feel powerless because you have the power to take steps that trigger your dopamine, serotonin, and oxytocin.

When you fall in the mud, your Personal Agency circuit reminds you that you have fallen into mud before and successfully pulled yourself out. People have fallen into mud all through human history and gotten out. "It's worse this time," your cortisol tells you. Instead of focusing on that "something is wrong" feeling, you can focus on your next step. You can stay open to new information. New expectations will build.

While you're stuck in the mud, you may see people stepping past you on the rocks. You may think they have good rocks and you have bad rocks. You may think the idiots in power should have built a bridge over the river. You may think crisis is inevitable. You look for social support, and discover that everyone around you is talking about crisis and stupid leaders and bad rocks. With your attention focused on these things, you see no way to move forward. But when you shift your attention to the details in front of you, you see a small foothold.

Your brain lacks the bandwidth to curse the river and cross it at the same time. Invest your bandwidth in your next best step and you will like the results. Each step has value whether you are one step away from your goal or far from it. Persevere and you'll get where you're going.

Your Own Best Agent

Chances are you're not going to find yourself literally stuck in the mud anytime soon. But you can use the PARE habit to move forward in your real life situations, too.

When things are harder than I expected, I think about my husband's parking karma. My husband is "lucky" at parking. I wondered how he did it, and realized that he grabs the first spot available instead of circling around for a "good" spot. He never breaks the law or steals from others. He just anticipates opportunities and is pleased with what he finds. I decided to be "lucky," too. I no longer hesitate on the assumption that I'll find something better. Instead of wasting energy circling, I take what I find and feel pleased with my decision.

In truth, I sometimes have a long walk from my "good" parking spot. I may even pass better spots, and I'm tempted to criticize myself for not doing better. Then, I quickly activate my positivity circuit—the one that says walking is better than circling. I decide to feel good about my choices instead of investing my energy in endless optimizing. I've done this so many times now that I start expecting to feel good about my choices. So I do.

You should keep in mind that it feels great when you finally cross a river or get a "good" parking space, but the feeling doesn't last. Your mind will notice an even greener pasture on the far side of yet another river. No bridge is there, but you decide to give it a try and go to that greener pasture. The risks and rewards are hard to predict, but you keep updating your information and focusing on your next step. You are positive!

Science Summary

Negativity is a real physical pathway in your brain, but you can build a positivity pathway instead. Your brain is always seeing the world through the lens of the pathways you have because it's impossible to process every detail around you. You may think positivity is "biased," but when you understand your inner mammal you realize that your negative lens was biased and in need of correction.

- Form a positivity habit by feeding your brain with a new stream of inputs. Three times a day, stop and think of something good that's going on in your life.

- You are ultimately your own agent. You make the hard decisions and you deal with the consequences. You can enjoy the act of being your own agent instead of focusing on inevitable disappointments.

- Your efforts often fail to have immediate visible results, so it helps to know that they often have long-run effects you can't see. It's natural to be discouraged when you don't see results, but most human good has come from efforts that did not get immediate visible results.

- When you get what you seek, it feels like the world is under control. But that's not realistic, and if you expect it you will end up feeling like the world is out of control.

- Taking steps toward meeting your needs feels good. It's tempting to delay your steps until you find a path of complete certainty because the human cortex can imagine such a path. But the real world will never meet this expectation, so it's good to know that your inner mammal is designed to meet needs by taking one step at a time.

THE PATHWAY TO A
POSITIVE
BRAIN

Train your brain to recognize positivity and
embrace solutions.

You've probably been hearing that the world is on the brink of collapse all your life. You can surely list ten crises in ten seconds. Our world certainly has threats that require attention, but humans are still here because problems keep getting solved. No one seems to feel good about successful problem-solving, however. A sense of doom is more common.

"Nothing can fix it now," people say. They see the world through crisis goggles of their own making. In this chapter, you'll find positive ways to handle these perceived threats. Here is support for the positivity soapbox, if you dare to step on it. No solutions are prescribed—just a way to focus on solutions instead of on crisis. You can be realistic and transcend negativity, even in the face of heckling.

CRISIS GOGGLES

If you point your finger randomly at a timeline of human history, you will be pointing at a time when people said, "Things are bad these days and the idiots in charge don't know what they're doing." Chances are you are hearing that right now. The crisis-mongers around you may say, "This time it's different. Now, those idiots have *really* messed up." It's hard to avoid crisis goggles, for all these reasons:

- You know you will die. The end is near indeed from the perspective of your mortal body. You don't think that consciously, but reminders of your mortality trigger threat chemicals that tell your brain to look for threats.

- A mammal feels threatened when its group-mates feel threatened. Shared crisis goggles create the nice sense of belonging that mammals seek. You risk losing these bonds if you ignore the alarm calls of your group-mates, so there's a strong incentive to feel threatened when others do.

- Reporting threats brings social rewards, so we hear a lot of threat reports. Our brains habituate to old threats, so people have to report bigger threats to get the rewards. Such reports surround us in fiction (movies, television shows, literature) and nonfiction (news, politics, research), and we can easily add our own threat reports through social media.

- You may have been taught that crisis is good because it helps destroy the old "bad" society, and make way for the new "better world." This perspective trains you to expect crisis, and your cortex can easily find evidence to meet this expectation. Unfortunately, the expecation of rewards at the end of the crisis distracts you from seeing more positive alternatives to crisis.

- Cortisol tells your cortex to look for evidence of threat. Your cortex is good at finding what it looks for. When you feel bad, it finds something bad to explain the feeling.

- When you say, "Things are worse now than ever" you are forgetting how things were in the past. And even if you did learn how things were in the distant past, the events described in history books don't trigger your threat chemicals the way present frustrations do. Today's challenges always feel worse, even when you have all of the historical facts and those facts say otherwise.

Many people think their sense of crisis is a way to "help." They even speak harshly of those who do not share their sense of crisis. They may accuse you of "not helping" if you take off your crisis goggles.

But you can take them off anyway.

You can enjoy a sense of accomplishment instead of a sense of crisis. When you hear people discuss the state of the world, you can remember that they are mammals. Their brains are trying to stimulate happy chemicals and avoid pain in ways that worked for them before. It's not easy being a mammal. But you can teach your inner mammal to focus on the positive, whether others do or not.

The **Mammal Brain** Says . . .

It's not easy being a mammal. But you can teach your inner mammal to focus on the positive, whether others do or not.

Each of us chooses what to do with our brain, regardless of what others choose. The positive choice is uncommon so it's hard to imagine it. Here is a simple thought experiment that helps. Imagine empty soapboxes at Speakers' Corner in London. Imagine yourself stepping onto one soapbox and saying, "Things are going to hell in a handbasket." Now, go to the other soapbox and say, "We will solve our problems." Does the hell-in-a-handbasket soapbox feel more comfortable? Do you feel more exposed to ridicule when you espouse problem-solving? Do you imagine being seen as intelligent and compassionate when you warn of looming crisis, but being heckled when you proclaim a positive future? It's easy to imagine hecklers saying "What about the climate crisis?" "What about the economic crisis?" "What about the social crisis?" Let's take a look at how you can focus on solutions instead of standing on a cynical soapbox.

WHAT ABOUT THE CLIMATE CRISIS?

When I was young, black smoke spewed from my car and black sludge flowed into my local waterways.

When my grandmother was young, coal dust left a black film in her home and in her lungs. Black sludge pooled around her home because there were no pipes to take it to the river.

Today, we worry about carbon dioxide emissions because dirtier emissions have been stopped. We are free to worry about long-term threats because more immediate threats have been managed. We worry about plastic ending up in the water, and we should. But more toxic stuff used to go into the water. We can appreciate the improvement. Many people think it's helpful to ignite a sense of crisis about pollution. But doing this obscures the extraordinary success of anti-pollution steps in recent decades. Ignoring extraordinary success is not helpful.

A "do something" feeling about our planet is useful, but it can be a positive feeling rather than a negative feeling. It's not realistic to expect unlimited resources, so conserving natural resources is realistic. Each person can take steps to use fewer resources. You can do that without feeling any anger at the system or harboring fear of imminent doom. You can do it with good feelings such as efficiency or creativity.

This is hard to do when your information is all negative. Here is some positive information about sustainability, which can help put the negatives in context.

A Declining Population

World population is forecast to start declining in a few decades. This is a colossal achievement. Some insist it won't happen fast enough to prevent collapse. Others insist it will happen too fast and cause economic collapse. That negativity buries the great news. Let us pause instead to appreciate the magnitude of this accomplishment. We have taken a brain that cares mostly about reproduction and taught it to limit reproduction to replacement levels. Going below replacement levels temporarily will help sustainability even more. This is great news. If you twist it into bad news, that's a habit you can transcend.

Corporations Are Mammalian Social Alliances

I often hear that the Earth is threatened by evil corporations bent on world domination. Casting corporations in the role of predator and bully helps the mammal brain make sense of the world. It helps us explain our mammalian frustrations with social dominance. It helps us bond around common enemies, and vent at safe targets instead of lethal predators. Blaming threats on corporations gives your mammal brain the nice, safe feeling of knowing where threats are coming from. But it limits your information so it doesn't really make you safer. When you understand your inner mammal, you know that corporations are mammalian social alliances just like any other. Every group of mammals faces similar dynamics, including the groups you belong to. I have learned to ignore the constant blare of predator alarm calls and choose my own information.

Sustainability Expectations

Today's sustainability consciousness is a huge accomplishment. In the past, people exploited the Earth's resources to survive, and animals did, too. Harmony with nature is a figment of the poetic imagination. For example, we hear that elephants help the environment because their dung creates soil, but elephants destroy their environment at a much faster rate. Elephants don't restrain their impulse to consume nature faster than it regenerates, but humans are learning just such restraint. Humans hunted as much as they could in the past, but today the killing of wild animals has been regulated all over the world. The regulations are not yet enforced everywhere, so there's more to be done. We can do it better with realistic expectations.

WHAT ABOUT THE ECONOMIC CRISIS?

When my mother was young, she worried about the food running out before payday. When her grandmother was young, people worried about food running out before the next harvest. When I was young, I worried about getting hungry away from home, and I carried snacks instead of wasting money on restaurant food. I wrote letters home from college instead of wasting money on long-distance phone calls. I grew up in a home with one bathroom and one television and one phone. The official poverty line is higher today, but I felt rich because I got to keep the money from my after-school jobs instead of using it to help support my family.

When I left home, I lived in apartments with moldy, decaying surfaces in the kitchens and bathrooms, but I was thrilled to have my own space. When I got my first job, I bought some things that broke in a short time, but I was thrilled to have another paycheck coming. And when my job felt wrong, I was glad that I knew how to live cheaply, and so I could quit.

Talk about economic crisis has become so pervasive that people seem to reflexively associate the economy with pain. They blame the economy for the sting of social disappointment that is part of every mammal's life. It is not realistic to expect the economy to make you happy, because the mammal brain is always seeking. Here are some ways to feel good about the economy and transcend the bad feelings.

Positivity at Work

We want work to be fun. It's often not fun because we feel judged. It's easy to feel like your survival is threatened when your work is judged, even though you judge the work of others all the time. All this workplace judging benefits us in ways we rarely notice. The quality of goods and services has risen, but our expectation that everything be perfect every time means we live with strict quality controls at work. If your bank makes an error, you get upset, but you don't notice the bank's billions of correct transactions. If a restaurant makes a mistake, someone gets upset, but if it serves a hundred meals beautifully, that's taken for granted. We don't feel good about the high-quality standards we enjoy because we're busy looking for defects and feeling judged. The "zero defect" strategy for quality control teaches that every defect is a crisis. I taught this strategy when I was a management professor, and now I wish I had taught people to notice how much is working right as well as the occasional wrong.

Positivity about Money

People fear running out of money in old age. Yet expectations about the cost of aging can grow unrealistically. If you need assisted living, the cost will include specialists with master's degrees who will urge you to stay active. It will include staffers to pick up any tissue you might drop because you will not be permitted to bend over and pick it up yourself. And if you happen to bend over and fall, they will take you to the emergency room whether you feel hurt or not. Extreme measures become "necessities" when organizations fear lawsuits. Such inflation has permeated every life stage, from birth to death. In the past, people navigated life's stages without expert guidance. But today, it seems too dangerous to manage birth, education, career, marriage, and aging without lots of expert services. If you spent your life worrying about the right school, the right job, and the right house, you will probably worry about the right nursing home. That's not the economy's fault. Worrying about your money running out before you die is a distraction from the real fear that you will be gone before the money is. The economy can't fix that for you, so instead of focusing on the pain at the end of the road, you can focus on the pleasure of the steps along the way.

Positivity about Social Status

Every mammal wants respect, and today we often seek it through career. The quest is so frustrating that we don't realize how much worse it was in the days when you got respect by winning fist fights, by having as many babies as possible, or by joining a rigid hierarchy (like a priesthood, army, or aristocracy). The mammal brain releases a great feeling of social dominance when your job status rises. When you don't get the career advancement you expected, it feels like a survival threat. The threatened feelings stay with you, but the good feelings pass as your attention shifts to the next goal. Your mammal brain will keep seeking status and noticing threats. The economy did not cause this and it cannot give you a constant serotonin high.

Positivity about Progress

Progress is widely used as a bad word. People are so quick to focus on the negative side of progress that they ignore the pain that came before the progress. You may imagine your ancestors in a Garden of Eden, living effortlessly off the fat of the land. Researchers feed this fantasy and evidence to the contrary gets ignored. Our ancestors lived with food shortages, invasions, and plagues, a lot. They rarely had a "job" in the sense of an income guaranteed by someone else. A farmer or craftsman lived with the constant risk of not producing enough to meet their survival needs. Today, we expect employers to bear that risk, and instead of feeling good about it, employers are often resented. I learned to sympathize with employers because my father once hired someone and had to pay them when he couldn't pay himself. He paid them even when he lost money on them. Surviving on what you sell or produce each day is a huge threat to live with. The cubicle life frees you from that threat, but you probably take it for granted.

Positivity about Disappointment

Disappointment is inevitable with a brain that filters the world through its own expectations. For example, when you sell your used car, it's easy to have high expectations and get disappointed. But if you were buying that same car, it would be easy to have low expectations and get disappointed. You can end up disappointed all the time, and if you don't understand the bias in your expectations, you could think "the free market" is the source of your frustrations. You might blame "the system" for keeping prices low one day and for keeping prices high another day without even noticing the contradiction. It's comforting to have an external enemy to make sense of your internal sense of threat, but that just expands your sense of threat in the end. It's natural to long for a system that favors sellers when you're a seller and buyers when you're a buyer, but it's not realistic. With realistic expectations, you can enjoy being your own agent whether you're a buyer or seller despite the brain's inevitable bias. Whether you're in the market for a car, a house, a job, or a vinyl Elvis recording, you can learn to go positive instead of going negative.

Positivity about Food

Humans have worried about food since they've had enough neurons to worry. In the past, food supplies were threatened by nature, vermin, and aggressive neighbors. Today, these threats have been managed so well that our brains scan for new threats. Though we enjoy unprecedented food security, many people feel intense threat about food. The quest for optimum health turns every food choice into a matter of life and death. The daily pressure to improve nutrition leads to a sense of crisis about "the food system." The positive side of our food economy is widely overlooked. I once found a worm in the dried apricots I bought in an exotic open market on a trip abroad. I had been eating those apricots for days. I used to be cynical about American food packaging, but I suddenly understood the reasons for it. Before food was packaged, people needed pet snakes to keep rats away from their food. Before packaging, worm eggs in your food ended up in your stomach. Packaging solved real problems. I don't eat packaged food anymore because secure bulk food is now available, but I do appreciate the new options instead of getting angry about the old options.

Where I live, anger at the food industry is intense. But when I buy food, I appreciate the colossal effort it takes to fill up a store with unspoiled food. I know how quickly food spoils once you bring it home. And yet, when I want an ingredient that I only use rarely, an unspoiled supply is there for me. I marvel at that logistical miracle instead of sneering at it.

I often see fruit vendors lined up on the street when I travel abroad. Each vendor stands all day with a small pile of fruit. This seems so inefficient that I was pleased to find an economist who had studied it. He interviewed market women and learned that a huge chunk of their earnings was spent on the bus ticket that brought them in from their village with their produce. Childcare also cost a lot because they'd sleep at the market each night until their produce sold out. "Why don't you just send one person with all the crops?" he asked. They told him, "I wouldn't trust anyone to give me my fair share." That helped me understand the value of accounting and legal systems. I even appreciate fixed prices since I hate bargaining for each piece of fruit. Modern commerce improves your life in ways you can understand if you go beyond cynical thinking.

WHAT ABOUT THE SOCIAL CRISIS?

When my grandparents came to America, other immigrants from their Sicilian village clustered on one street in Brooklyn. They didn't trust people from other parts of Sicily who lived on other streets in Brooklyn. And these Sicilians didn't trust immigrants from other parts of Italy.

My parents went to schools and churches with people from a wide range of cultures. I used to think my parents were inbred because they married other Italians, but I learned that they had married outside their province (mother's family was from Naples!), and that was rarely done by their ancestors. Their grandparents hardly met anyone from outside their village.

Circles of trust expanded over time. Restaurants invented the concept of "Italian food," combining the traditions of people who rarely spoke to each other before. Today, restaurants serve dishes from countries that warred with each other for generations. I see people from warring cultures sit at adjacent tables without incident. I celebrate this accomplishment instead of taking it for granted. Evidence of social harmony is everywhere, but you don't see it if you focus on conflict.

I live near winding roads with little room for passing traffic, yet drivers stop and let each other pass all day without incident. Drivers of every human variety manage tons of steel with remarkable safety.

Occasionally, a driver gives me a threatened feeling, but if I focused on that I would miss so much good.

The massive expansion of social trust is widely overlooked. For most of human history, it was not safe to leave your village, and you stuck to your network of "introductions" if you dared to venture beyond it. Today, you can wander far from home in unprecedented safety. I have wandered into many massage studios in China, and had a fabulous, skillful treatment every time. It's a miracle that I can walk in off the street on the other side of the world and entrust my safety to strangers. I never stop appreciating it.

Rising Expectations

The perception of social crisis is caused by rising expectations, which makes things look worse as they get better. For example, domestic violence is now seen as intolerable where it used to be seen as "a private matter." Great progress is made when domestic violence goes from "don't talk about it" to "find it and fight it." The progress can't be measured because there's no reliable data on the "before" situation when people refused to talk about it. Progress is often downplayed by "activists," who strive to create a continual sense of crisis. Advocacy groups broaden the definition of a problem, and they condemn talk of improvement as "insensitive." This makes the world look bleaker as things improve.

The world is full of people who are eager to help others. But help doesn't always "help." It can even make things worse when "help" rewards behaviors that perpetuate a problem. Cynics condemn humanity for presumed indifference. Instead, we can feel good about pervasive good intentions while building realistic expectations about help.

Social conflict preoccupies us because the mammal brain evolved to monitor it. Your mammal brain will keep comparing you to others and reacting. This impulse is stimulated by the proliferation of media. Disappointment can increase even as things improve because media give you the impression that everyone else is enjoying an ice cream and a foot rub all the time. No matter what you have, someone has something you lack and your mammal brain will notice. If you spun a globe and pointed anywhere, your finger would rest on a place where people are saying, "Our society is bad . . . and those idiots over there are even worse." Social tension is part of being a mammal. The world is never going to change in ways that make your mammal brain happy all the time. Fortunately, you have the power to manage your mammal brain.

The **Human Brain** Says . . .

Social conflict preoccupies us because the mammal brain evolved to monitor it. Your mammal brain will keep comparing you to others and reacting.

CHRONOCENTRISM

People say we're at a turning point in history. Every human who has ever lived has felt this way. Each brain sees its own time as special because that's the time you can do something about. People say the survival of life on Earth depends on us. It feels good to imagine your actions having an impact on the future. It feels even better to think future generations are on your side in your war with "the bad guys."

But this nice sense of historical significance can magnify your mammalian sense of threat. If you search the past and future for evidence of threat, that's what you will find. The brain stores information in reference to its needs. It sees the past as the lead-up to what matters to you today. It sees the future as the opportunity for your unique individual essence to spread. You don't think this consciously, of course, but it's hard to think otherwise.

Your brain's urge to predict rewards and threats is constantly frustrated because the world is not predictable. Future threats seem more ominous than past threats because you already know how the past story ends. Your future story is uncertain except for the fact that you will die, and if you have children, they will die. It feels like the world's survival is at stake because your survival is at stake.

When you accept your brain's interest in your own legacy, it helps you manage your sense of crisis. If you acknowledge concern for your personal apocalypse, it helps you make sense of the "do something" feeling. That feeling eases when you work to build something that can survive you. When you see other people strive to build a legacy, you may think it's pompous or trivial, but you are the center of the world for your brain, and you have to work with the brain you've got.

Science Summary

Your brain finds it easy to see signs of crisis because incessant talk of crisis builds those circuits. You can enjoy a positive view of the "crises" that disturb you instead.

- You can teach your inner mammal to focus on the positive whether others do or not.

- A "do something" feeling about our planet is useful, but it can be a positive feeling rather than a negative feeling. This is hard to do when your information is all negative. Fortunately, there is positive information about sustainability, which can help put the negatives in context.

- Talk about economic crisis has become so pervasive that people seem to reflexively associate the economy with pain. But it is not realistic to expect the economy to make you happy because the mammal brain is always seeking.

- The mammal brain is designed to compare itself to others and to release a bad feeling when it sees itself in the one-down position. As much as you try to avoid this bad feeling, it keeps coming back because you can't be in the one-up position every moment. Humans have lived with social frustration since the beginning of time, and if your other needs are met, you may focus on it relentlessly. It will feel like a crisis and your brain will find evidence that fits. Of course you will end up feeling worse. Fortunately, you can learn to take off the crisis goggles and find ways of feeling good about your place in the world.

- It feels good to imagine your actions having an impact on the future. It feels even better to think future generations are on your side in your war with "the bad guys." But this nice sense of historical significance can magnify your mammalian sense of threat. If you search the past and future for evidence of threat, you will end up with an endless sense of threat. You have the power to see an alternative future instead.

AFTERWORD

When I was in college, most countries in the world were ruled by dictators who imprisoned and tortured those who didn't submit. I was constantly told of the suffering these dictators caused. Then, almost miraculously, those dictators fell within a short span of time and democracies sprang up to replace them. This positive turn of events was beyond my wildest dreams. I was thrilled, but no one around me seemed happy about it. They had already shifted to the next crisis. So instead of celebrating, I embraced the negativity that surrounded me.

Since that time, I have watched dozens of crises come and go. I have noticed the way people pride themselves on their ability to find evidence of crisis. And I realized that I would never feel good if I waited for the people around me to feel good. You may think it's wrong to feel good while others are suffering, but if that were true, no one in human history could ever have felt good.

You may think it's delusional to focus on good when evidence of suffering is everywhere. But the dog poop rule can help us be realistic. When 80 percent of pet owners let their dogs mess on the streets, we take that mess for granted, but when 20 percent of pet owners let their dogs mess on the streets, we say "what is wrong with this world!" We humans solve problems because our mammal brain creates a sense of urgency, which sends our intelligent cortex looking for new information. There will always be problems, a feeling of urgency, and a quest for new information. It will never be the right time to feel good unless you make it your personal mission to do so. I hope you will do it now instead of waiting as long as I did.

APPENDIX:
PERSONAL AGENCY IN
BOOKS AND MOVIES

You can balance the cynicism around you by seeking out positive inputs. In this appendix you'll find suggestions for books, TV shows, and movies about inspirational real people who had Personal Agency and Realistic Expectations (PARE). Their focus was not on fighting the system, but on navigating the steps it takes to build something. They will help you see problem-solving as more than a David-versus-Goliath battle and instead as an experiment with unknown results. Turn to these stories when you want to keep your perspective positive.

The heroes of these stories had plenty of setbacks. They lived with frustration and uncertainty as they built what we now take for granted. When you hear about the obstacles in their lives, it's tempting to get angry at "the system." Yet these people stayed focused on the details of the problem, transcended their mammalian negativity, and kept building despite the uncertainty of social rewards.

MOVIES

Life Story

This recent wildlife documentary by David Attenborough encapsulates our mammalian inheritance in a beautiful format. It explores the life story that every living creature has in common, from birth to genetic immortality, with images of unprecedented quality. The most moving hour of the six is hour number four, called "Power." It illuminates the animal struggle for social dominance with such elegance that you will be able to accept this fact of life instead of clinging to the comfortable idea that "our society" causes the urge for power.

Many people are familiar with Attenborough's voice without knowing his historic role in our understanding of nature. He is not just a talking head. He has pioneered documentation of behavior in the wild since the 1950s. He continually spearheaded technical advances that allowed deeper knowledge of survival behavior to emerge. And he did this without submitting to the fashionable habit of romanticizing animals and vilifying humans. He provides accurate depictions of the conflict among animals, which helps us understand and manage our inner mammal instead of externalizing our internal impulses. Sir David's fascinating personal story is told in a book and video entitled *Life Stories*, so the reader is cautioned to distinguish between the two titles.

Longitude

If you've ever felt mistreated by bureaucracy, you will love this story of an inventor who was denied prize money he'd rightfully won. This TV miniseries is based on the book *Longitude: The True Story of a Lone Genius Who Solved the Greatest Scientific Problem of His Time*. Today, global positioning is taken for granted, but in 1714, ships got lost at sea because there was no way for sailors to measure their longitude. The British Parliament offered a prize for a workable method to help their ships return safely to harbor.

One solution was to build a clock that kept perfect time on long sea voyages. A country carpenter set out to build such a clock. John Harrison's creation was extremely accurate when tested on jostling oceans, but the award committee disdained it. He kept improving his invention, making better clocks into his sixties and seventies, but the committee kept snubbing him. Finally he complained to King George III, and at age eighty he was awarded the prize money (though not the official prize).

Harrison was snubbed for a typically mammalian reason: The award-committee leaders were protecting their turf. They were astronomers, and Harrison's invention made it possible to navigate without astronomy. Any uneducated carpenter or sailor could measure longitude with his gadget, which diminished the value and prestige of an astronomer's skill.

The movie obscures this point a bit. It shows the scientists of the Royal Society in wigs and robes as they brand Harrison "not one of us." The educated elite did not want the biggest problem of their time to be solved by a mere "mechanic," so they kept changing the rules to make sure he lost. But it wasn't just his country clothing and country speech that threatened them. It was his power to lower their status by raising the status of something new.

Your new idea may have been snubbed by turf protectors. But you may have resisted new ideas yourself. Our careers come to rest on a particular method, and we are not always happy to see a new thing come along. It's easy to hate the guys in wigs when you watch the movie without noticing that when you are that guy, you too might very well sneer at something that threatens to make you obsolete. Every new method must prove itself, and turf wars raise the bar on that proof.

John Harrison triumphed in the end because he kept building better clocks. Those clocks are now on display in London. You can go see them at the Greenwich Royal Observatory, where you can take your picture stepping on the Prime Meridian as you exit. You can also watch the Harrison clocks on YouTube videos.

There's another story about this incident that's inspiring as well. These clocks were left in a closet gathering dust for 150 years. They are available for our enjoyment today because of the persistence of another individual whose story is included in the *Longitude* video. A soldier suffering shell shock in World War I found the clocks in a closet while recuperating at the Greenwich Naval Hospital. He understood their significance and spent years restoring them to working order. His story underscores the fact that we have good things around us because people who came before us invested tremendous effort.

October Sky

October Sky is based on the true story of a high-school student named Homer Hickam who teaches himself to build rockets. He was trying to help America respond to Sputnik, and he also wanted to escape from an unpleasant home life. This is a buddy movie where the buddies teach each other physics. The boy, played by a very young Jake Gyllenhaal, meets harsh resistance from his own father. The young rocket scientist tackles a long string of obstacles with amazing panache (this is an autobiography, admittedly) and his rockets fly miles into the air.

Hickam's skill was in cultivating allies—classmates, teachers, mechanics, and townspeople—as much as achievements in rocket science. It's charming to see him build the support he needs. New roadblocks keep appearing and Homer keeps surmounting them. Then word of mouth spreads, and ever-growing crowds attend the West Virginia rocket launches.

Homer's father feels responsible for safety because he's chief of the mine that employs most of the town. A mishap could destroy Homer Senior's career. As much as we want to hate him for obstructing progress, we can easily see that the rocket launches are dangerous and would never be allowed today. Dad seems to have neglected his family except for Homer's football-hero brother. Homer Junior suffers acutely from the disrespect of his father and older brother, even as he gets growing respect from the town. Our deepest pain often comes from those closest to us. This is made even more clear in the book version of Homer Hickam's autobiography (first published as *Rocket Boys*). (Hickam also wrote a series of young adult books.)

The family-friendly movie distorts the book by forcing it into an up-from-poverty mold. Poverty is not keeping Homer from going to college. His own father vetoes college unless Homer agrees to go into the mining biz. Homer transcends the negativity by focusing on building something. He takes big steps and learns from mistakes—both science mistakes and social mistakes. The rocket boys don't complain about the inadequacy of school budgets and science curricula. They just keep putting one foot in front of another.

In one scene in the book, Homer slices an artery on the scrap metal he's collecting to raise funds for supplies. His friends fear he will bleed to death if they leave him, so they force him to make the 3-mile walk back to town. There, the doctor sews him up without anesthesia, and scolds him while doing it. When Homer finally gets home, his mother makes him shower off the junkyard smell before going to bed, and scolds him while he's showering. This contrasts sharply with today's culture of withholding criticism and giving young people big strokes for little effort. When children and teens are unmotivated, we often blame the world for not stroking them enough. Sometimes they learn to blame the world instead of taking realistic personal action. This book evokes another way of thinking. It's cruel indeed, and we've done well to transcend it, but it also reminds us to find our strength.

The King's Speech

Queen Elizabeth's father was a stutterer, and public speaking was the last thing he wanted to do. This is the story of King George VI's efforts to overcome his speech impediment and perform the role fate had cast him in. A talented speech therapist helps him build new circuits in the muscles that control speech and breathing. This movie shows how hard it is to rewire yourself, no matter who you are.

If you were a king, you would still be a mammal. You would feel the sting of cortisol when reminded of past hurts. George VI had lots of cortisol circuits because he grew up with a lot of cruelty. He learned to fear people more than trust them, and so his internal alarm blared when he spoke. This movie makes you feel the king's powerlessness as he struggles with the quirky operating system of a brain he built long ago.

The speech therapist is the hero of the movie. Lionel Logue leads the king instead of taking the subordinate role. He doesn't let the king escape from pain by pulling rank. We have all been tempted to run when change is uncomfortable, so you can imagine how tempting that would be if you were king. Logue keeps pushing George to face the internal challenge, so the movie appeals to our mammalian urge to one-up the alpha.

The book shows complexity that's not in the movie. Lionel Logue left diaries and letters that his grandson built into the book, *The King's Speech: How One Man Saved the British Monarchy*. Logue said in his journal that the king worked harder at the exercises Logue designed than anyone he'd ever known. The book shows that Logue and George were not really "pals." The king rewarded Logue with generous fees, referrals, respect, and gratitude. But Logue's admiring grandson seems to think more (perhaps a knighthood?) was in order.

It's easy to see why the king would not want to call attention to his speech impediment by heroizing Logue in public.

The book also describes Logue's continual efforts to connect with the king over the years. You could call it "friendship," but it was more like the normal networking that professionals do. Logue was a skilled professional who did not need the king's friendship to survive. Each man was his own agent, and they formed an alliance that was extremely effective for both of them.

Romantics Anonymous

This is the tale of two compulsively shy French people who find love while selling chocolate. It explores social anxiety with humor that's never mean-spirited. As the characters confront their negative expectations, we are always laughing with them rather than at them. In the end (spoiler alert) they create a great relationship and a great business by transcending their fears.

The French title of the movie, *Les émotifs anonymes*, describes it well. Emotions Anonymous is an international 12-step program for people seeking to resolve anxiety, depression, or low self-esteem in a structured group context. The group supports the heroine of the movie as she timidly finds a job, dates her boss, and turns around his company. The boss is terrified of her, but he makes overtures because his therapist assigned it as homework. When she responds favorably, he's even more terrified. He doesn't blame society for his anxiety. He says, "I'm scared," and focuses on the thing he has power over: himself.

Anxiety is natural because the mammal brain keeps retrieving old disappointments in an effort to avoid new disappointments. It's hard to take steps toward rewards when you expect disappointment. The characters in this story take the steps anyway, and gradually build new expectations. The movie is a very enjoyable way to go beyond cynicism.

The Sicilian Girl

This is a dark story about a girl who stood up to the Mafia. It's a brilliant depiction of herd behavior. Leaving the herd is a survival threat in a Mafia community, so the character's fear is realistic.

The movie's heroine violates the famous Mafia code of silence. Her father and brother are murdered in front of her eyes, so she decides to join the anti-Mafia herd instead. Everyone she knows shuns her, including her mother. The girl puts her trust in a famous Italian prosecutor, but he cannot even protect himself.

The movie is based on the true story of Rita Atria, whose father and brother were not innocent victims but Mafiosi themselves. The murders Rita witnessed were part of a revenge cycle. As the movie shows, if someone in your trusted in-group threatens you, your brain faces a terrible dilemma. You're threatened if you stay and threatened if you leave. We learn by watching, and we often see those around us avoid conflict by ignoring an internal threat and focusing on an external one.

BOOKS

Darwin's Ghosts: The Secret History of Evolution

The ghosts of the title are people who understood evolution before Charles Darwin. Darwin's predecessors did not completely figure out natural selection, but they realized that the endless variation of species was caused by survival-promoting adaptation over time. One of the "ghosts" was Darwin's own grandfather, Erasmus Darwin, who died before Charles was born. Erasmus was a doctor but he explained evolution in a long poem on nature in hopes of making it more accessible. This book reminds us that our efforts are not wasted. Someone will inherit your work and do something with it.

Darwin's teen self is included as one of the "ghosts." We meet young Charles as a college student at the beach. He was there because he didn't like school and he liked to collect marine life. Darwin was in medical school at his father's insistence, but he had no stomach for it. At the beach, he met other budding naturalists. One of them said, "You're the grandson of Erasmus Darwin?" Charles thus came to recognize the importance of his grandfather's obscure work, and it showed him a way to get respect by doing what he loved.

Long before the Darwins, speculation about the mutation of species had come from Ancient Greece, Islamic scholars, the American frontier, and French philosophy. This book includes information on the individuals who looked at the world with fresh eyes. They didn't have fMRI brain scans or electron microscopes for molecular genetics, but they watched animals mate and plants propagate, and studied the outcome. In Darwin's day, the selective breeding of livestock and plants was an important economic activity and a popular hobby. Hereditary biology was widely understood before the mechanics of genetic transmission were known.

Today, people still interpret evolution through the lens of their prior beliefs. For example, I am surrounded by people who think it's bad to eat meat, and so the role of hunting in the evolutionary process has become an unmentionable. It's easy to see that the human brain grew big as more animal protein and fat became available. Better hunting led to bigger brains, which led to even better hunting and bigger brains. Scholars who disdain hunting approve of collectivism, so they will allow that collectivist food-seeking led to more food, more brain growth, and thus more collectivism. But the meat is an unmentionable.

Similarly, sexual selection is widely overlooked. Evolution is driven by mating choices as much as by genetic mutations. But animal mating behavior conflicts with progressive gender ideals in many ways. People would rather not talk about it. They emphasize genetic mutations instead, which leads to the apocalyptic view that an old species must die out for a better-adapted species to replace it. The more benign truth is that sexual selection spreads adaptive traits without the need for mass die-offs. Animals simply seek out mates with characteristics that happen to promote survival in their niche. Politically incorrect male and female mating behaviors drive evolution, but it's not nice to say so.

In my world today, evolution is often used as a weapon in a battle with religion or a battle to save animals. When science becomes a weapon in a battle, something is lost. *Darwin's Ghosts* portrays science as an openness to observation regardless of the social consequences.

Wildlife Wars: My Fight to Save Africa's Natural Treasures

As poachers with AK-47s fanned out from conflict zones in Africa in the 1980s, African elephants were killed in great numbers. This is the story of Richard Leakey's efforts to stop it. His success angered powerful forces who were getting a slice of the ivory trade. Richard lost both of his legs in an apparent sabotage of the plane he piloted between wildlife reserves. Four months later, he was back at work, leading the Kenya Wildlife Service to resist the poachers. A photo in the book shows him leading on prosthetic legs. Now that's pretty positive!

Richard Leakey was born and raised in Kenya. He's the son of archeologists Louis and Mary Leakey, and an accomplished paleontologist in his own right. He was asked to lead the Kenya Wildlife Service (KWS) because he brought global attention to the plight of the elephants. At the time of his appointment, the KWS was highly corrupt. Revenue from park entrance fees and foreign aid disappeared into private pockets. Nothing was left to enforce the parks' boundaries or maintain the infrastructure so vital to tourism. If you ever wonder, "Why don't they do something to protect wildlife?" this book illuminates some of the obstacles for doing so.

Richard showed extraordinary strength in the face of staggering challenges. Corrupt officials kept protecting the poachers, and Richard's own brother was a member of the corrupt government. To complicate matters, that brother had donated the kidney that saved Richard's life years earlier. From family politics to world politics, the frustrations of being a mammal are realistically explored in this fascinating book.

Disclosing the Past

The "past" referred to in the title is both our specie's past and the personal past of paleontologist Mary Leakey, mother of Richard and wife of Louis. The Leakeys were known for finding fossils that revealed human origins in Africa. This book reminds us that Mary did most of the digging while her husband was out raising funds, networking, and generally acting like an alpha. Their partnership lasted for three decades, and they established the field of paleontology while raising three children in a harsh environment.

Mary had little formal education. She grew up following her father in the wilderness instead of going to school. He was a nomadically inclined painter of landscapes. When Mary was eleven, she lived in the Dordogne region of France, which is full of cave paintings. Her family developed close bonds with local collectors of early human artifacts, and Mary decided to become an archeologist. At the age her peers would finish high school, she went to London to make a place for herself in archeology. Her excellent drawing skills, learned from working with her father, made her valuable to field researchers in the days before digital photography and photocopying. Soon she was drawing for Louis Leakey.

Mary and Louis Leakey married and she followed him into the wilderness. But he continued to reach out to young ladies. His initiatives led to much of our knowledge of apes in the wild, because he sent Jane Goodall, Dian Fossey, and Birute Galdikas into the field to live alongside chimpanzees, gorillas, and orangutans, respectively. These women generated the first systematic knowledge of wild apes by devoting their lives to field research and conservation. Louis Leakey trained them and raised the funds that got them started, which is why they are sometimes referred to as "Leakey's Angels."

Mary's perspective on this story is a welcome addition. She ended up spending most of her life in Africa at extremely remote dig sites and her book gives credit to the roles that both she and her husband played. She kept her focus on empirical science while Louis focused on public science. Mary's book gives credit to both roles.

The Doctors' Plague: Germs, Childbed Fever, and the Strange Story of Ignác Semmelweis

You may know of Ignác Semmelweis, the nineteenth-century doctor who discovered that handwashing saves lives. You may know that he was berated and ignored by the medical establishment of his day. This book by accomplished surgeon and medical writer Sherwin Nuland defends the medical establishment. What possible defense could there be?

According to Nuland, Semmelweis did not "ask nicely" when he asked his fellow doctors to wash their hands. Nuland's view is quite upsetting when you first read it. After all, Dr. Ignác knew that mothers would die in agony and newborns would be orphaned when his advice was ignored. Who wouldn't be agitated? But the book raises an interesting point. The best thing Semmelweis could have done for those mothers would have been to present information in a way his fellow doctors could take in. Nuland was being realistic, and that's why this book is included here.

Germs were not known in Semmelweis's day. Doctors ridiculed the idea that "invisible animals" spread disease. Autopsies were the new fad for understanding disease, and obstetricians stayed busy doing autopsies while waiting for their patients to go into labor. They'd rush to the delivery room with hands full of matter from the last mother who died of infection. Mortality rates were extremely high in clinics staffed by doctors. Semmelweis brought that rate down to near zero by training his staff to wash with the best antiseptic available. He should have gotten respect. Why didn't he?

Let's consider the motivations of the mammals involved. Semmelweis could only prove his theory if his handwashing policy were enforced. He couldn't let doctors decide for themselves because deaths would then continue and there'd be no proof of the method. Strict enforcement was necessary, but it irked the doctors.

Once Semmelweis got his proof, he tried to spread the word quickly by writing letters to medical leaders throughout Europe. That seems like a reasonable response for his time, but it didn't work. Nuland explains this in a number of ways. First, Semmelweis failed to do laboratory research and publish results in the accepted style. When Louis

Pasteur and Joseph Lister did this, medical opinion changed quickly. Nuland suggests that Semmelweis was over-sensitive to rejection because of multiple professional rejections in his college years. Nuland raises a cultural issue as well. Semmelweis was a German-speaking Hungarian, and Nuland speculates that the German establishment dismissed him as Hungarian, while the Hungarians distrusted him for sounding German.

These are good arguments, but are they the whole story? Read this book and decide for yourself. In my opinion, Nuland overlooks the role of denial. No doctor wants to admit to being the cause of so many horrific deaths. Semmelweis was only motivated to admit it because of an accident of experience: his best friend died of "childbed fever" symptoms after cutting a finger during surgery. This helped Semmelweis focus on transmission rather than on childbirth as the cause. The personal pain of losing his friend triggered the cortisol that rewires a person quickly. Statistics on paper do not rewire people quickly.

By the time Lister and Pasteur came along, the germ theory of disease had been floating around for decades. In other words, the generation exposed to the idea of germs during their myelin years finally rose to power. Such a paradigm shift happens not because data accumulate, but because old alphas retire and get replaced by people who are exposed to the data while their brains were still in their years of peak neuroplasticity.

Poor Dr. Semmelweis went insane and died in a mental institution. More tragically still, he seems to have died of "childbed fever"—that is, a blood infection that began with an injury he sustained while brawling with the institution's staff on admission. When you read this book, it's easy to hate the medical gatekeepers who allowed the "doctor's plague" to continue. But you need to keep asking yourself, "What can I learn from Dr. Semmelweis?" Hating gatekeepers doesn't help.

Many people feel hostile toward the medical establishment today. It's natural to have a do-something feeling when disease threatens someone you love. Blaming doctors feels like doing something. We wish disease were more predictable, but it often takes generations for the truth about health and healing to sift out. George Washington died of a blood-letting that he commanded his doctor to perform. We all promote survival with the neural networks we happen to have.

Sometimes, urgent information gets buried due to career politics. When that happens, we often blame "our culture" or "our times." Nuland's book shows how this happened in another time and culture. This story helps us understand mammalian behavior instead of blaming the usual bad guys.

The Man Farthest Down: A Record of Observation and Study in Europe

A century ago, educator Booker T. Washington watched immigrants from Southern Europe pour into Alabama where he lived. He wondered what they were fleeing from that made them so eager to be there in Alabama. He planned a journey through Europe to find out. He determined to search for the "man at the bottom," whose condition in life was the worst of all. After touring many countries, he found what he deemed "the man farthest down" in Sicily. Perhaps he was focused on Italy because his biological father was descended from an Italian (the "T" stands for Taliaferro) who had immigrated to London generations earlier. Washington could write vividly of child labor in Italian mines because he had worked in West Virginia mines in his youth.

Booker T. Washington is a heroic transcender of cynicism. All of his books focus on improving one's next step rather than fighting enemies. Seeing Europe at the dawn of the twentieth century through his eyes is exciting, though the suffering he reports is sad. In this book, Washington keeps comparing the conditions he sees in Europe to the lives of African Americans, and concludes in each case that the European lives were much worse, which helps us understand the rigors of life a century ago. It's a great resource when people around you complain that life is hard "these days." When you realize how hard life was in Europe and the United States just a century ago, it helps you see the benefits of progress instead of reflexively bemoaning its curse.

Noble Savages: My Life Among Two Dangerous Tribes

Intellectual wars are fascinating because the emotion of primitive conflict lurks beneath the veneer of elevated discourse. This is the gripping story of anthropologist Napoleon Chagnon's war with the anthropology profession after the decades he spent in the Amazon among indigenous warring tribes. In the social sciences, the expectations of physical science are met in form, but in practice the data cannot be tested against physical reality as in the hard sciences. As a result, findings that fit widely shared expectations tend to get rewarded. The social sciences are united by the expectation that the state of nature is good, and "our society" is the source of all bad. Napoleon Chagnon dared to find bad in the state of nature—specifically, he found that a third of Yanomamo males die in conflicts with other tribesmen, and that the surviving warriors end up having more wives, more children, and thus more surviving copies of their genes. The alphas of anthropology declared war on him as a result. This book was very exciting for me because I spent most of my life in academia and witnessed mammalian social rivalry of this kind. I too have experienced the pressure to make the state of nature look good at the expense of the full facts. It was a pleasure to follow in Chagnon's steps as he resisted the temptation to follow the herd.

Country Driving: A Journey Through China from Farm to Factory

China recently experienced one of the biggest rural-to-urban migrations in human history and this book by Peter Hessler explores the choices of people who moved and of people who stayed. Many books focus on the suffering of Chinese workers, but this one focuses on their decision-making process. Hessler describes their efforts to navigate new opportunities, and his insights into human nature had me laughing out loud throughout the book.

Hessler went to China as a Peace Corps volunteer and stayed on as a journalist in Beijing. He rented a country cottage with a dirt floor and a view of the Great Wall to have a quiet place to write. The house is only two hours from Beijing, yet the country village it was in was almost abandoned in the rush to urbanize. Hessler's neighbors try to survive by serving foreign tourists who visit the Great Wall. But this section of the Wall is not restored, and middle-class Chinese on weekend getaways still see the village as a place to leave rather than a place to go. Hessler spends a lot of time with his neighbors, and tells us their story from each family member's perspective.

Driving around China was difficult in the past, so Hessler is excited by the chance to drive around the country. His road trips extend to a factory zone where he builds new relationships. He tells us about the lives of workers, managers, and entrepreneurs as they build new expectations and plot new strategies. The obstacles they face are unique in some ways but have much in common with mammals everywhere.

The Bookseller of Kabul

This book gives us the true story of a man who struggled for decades to keep books available in Kabul. He resisted the Soviets and then the Taliban with great courage. But he dominates his family as harshly as public authorities dominate him. A Norwegian journalist, Åsne Seierstad, who lived with the family for a long time wrote this book. In it she recounts the life and suffering of each family member in a very engaging way. The tragedy is that the very strength that enables the bookseller to stand up to public bullies makes him rather a bully at home. Each family member has a life that's utterly controlled by the family hierarchy, with almost no personal autonomy. You will not take your freedoms for granted after you read this book.

Intellectuals: From Marx and Tolstoy to Sartre and Chomsky

The juicy private lives of people revered by college professors are described in this book. The social dominance habits of Jean-Jacques Rousseau, Jean-Paul Sartre, Karl Marx, Percy Shelley, Henrik Ibsen, Leo Tolstoy, Ernest Hemingway, Bertolt Brecht, Bertrand Russell, Lillian Hellman, Norman Mailer, James Baldwin, and Noam Chomsky make for interesting reading. The pattern of self-serving, mean-spirited behavior toward colleagues, friends, and family was shocking, since these people presume to judge the rest of humanity. The frequency of addictions and other self-destructive behavior is also noteworthy in people who tell others how to live. Most troubling to read was their neglect of their own children, since these people made a lot of assertions in the name of "our children." This book reminded me that alpha status in the intellectual world is not as far removed from primal status conflicts as one might believe and it helped me feel good about my relative freedom from the dominance-seeking behavior that has always been such a part of the human experience.

Breaking Down the Wall of Silence: The Liberating Experience of Facing Painful Truth

Alice Miller wrote many books about the impact of early experience. Her work shows how child-rearing practices affect history, and how the childhood experience of a political leader can affect a nation. This volume includes the tragic story of Romania's Nicolae Ceaușescu, the Stalinist head of state known for the abusive orphanages that came to light after his era of mass atrocities. In the chapter aptly titled "The Monstrous Consequences of Denial," Miller shows how Ceaușescu and his wife reproduced the cruelties they suffered as children and inflicted them on the whole country. It's very disturbing, but everyone should read it to understand human nature. When I was in school I was taught to blame the misdeeds of humanity on the economic system. Today they might be blamed on genes. This book shows how evil deeds fit the template of early experience. We are not inevitably bound by our early experience, the author explains, because simple awareness of that template helps us recognize alternatives.

The Fortunate Pilgrim

Mario Puzo's autobiographical novel tells the story of a mother who pushes her children to earn money. You may think that means pushing them to study for high-wage professions, but it means, "Put the damned book down and get cash now." *The Fortunate Pilgrim* is the realistic book that Puzo wrote before he tried to write money-making blockbusters. He calls his mother a "fortunate pilgrim" because she keeps reminding her children how lucky they are to have opportunities in New York that they would not have in Italy. Puzo is honest about the anguish his mother caused. He does not present his family as good guys victimized by bad guys. That's a positive achievement by someone who clearly knows how to be cynical. This book provides a valuable way to understand how the need to eat has motivated young mammals to learn survival skills throughout human history.

Fortunately, Mario Puzo could resist his mother's expectations because he was the youngest child in his family, and his older siblings were already bringing in enough money to meet basic needs. One brother worked for the Mafia and this experience influenced Puzo's later works.

When *The Fortunate Pilgrim* flopped, Puzo wrote *The Godfather* to pay the bills. It's easy to see how Puzo's admiration of his older brother could lead to the sympathetic view of the Mafia expressed in *The Godfather*. Puzo has always insisted that his information came from research, but this highly autobiographical work suggests firsthand experience that he dared not mention. The success of *The Godfather* seems to rest on its cynicism. It indulges the core mammalian feeling that your social allies are the good guys no matter what they do. Violence is justified in the name of "family" and "loyalty." Social solidarity is so rewarding to the inner mammal that the ugliness associated with it is overlooked.

Studying monkeys and apes makes understanding the popularity of *The Godfather* a little easier to understand. You see, Puzo's characters put the nonverbal impulses of our primate ancestors into words. A classic example comes from the Godfather himself when he scorns a wedding guest who requests a murder. The Don is not against murder. He is only against the rudeness of asking for a favor without doing a favor first. He haughtily explains that the service is available to friends only. We have all experienced this conundrum of wanting a favor from someone we didn't bother to befriend before we wanted the favor, so it's fascinating to hear this nugget of etiquette verbalized by thugs. Don Corleone goes on to tell his guest what it takes to make "friends," and his expectations sound like the groomings and submission gestures that alpha monkeys expect from their troop-mates.

Paris Reborn

Many people look at Paris today and ask, "Why can't our cities look so good?" But if they lived in Paris when it was under construction in the mid-nineteenth century, they would probably have condemned the changes. Today's boulevards are there because old neighborhoods were sliced through. Today's architectural monuments are there because of status-seeking and budget overruns. *Paris Reborn* explains how things were built despite the acrimony.

Life would be easy if good things were created by good behavior, but Paris was created by the undemocratic and extravagant behavior of two people: Napoleon III and Baron Haussmann. Credit for building modern Paris usually goes to Haussmann, but the book shows that Louis-Napoleon supplied the vision and the drive. The nephew of Bonaparte (Napoleon I) was not the kind of person we would admire today. He took power in a coup and reigned through glitz and pageantry. But he was obsessed with the idea of making Paris modern. In about two decades, he built the first modern drinking water, sewer, and transportation systems in Paris, as well as most of the buildings that are iconic today.

If you had worked with Baron Haussmann, you probably would have found it unpleasant. He was power-seeking and wanted everything done his way. My favorite quote from the book is "Throughout the changes and course corrections, Haussmann mercilessly disparaged his predecessor while demonstrating his own prowess at overseeing the works." You have probably worked with people like that, and you may have felt they were ruining your life. But if you live long enough, you might one day flaunt your association with the Great One on the Great Project.

Napoleon III and Haussmann dominated their adversaries and made Paris into a tourist destination, which was a unique accomplishment at the time. We hate domineering leaders today, but many projects we love were hated at first. Endless criticism of new projects can paralyze, and the objections are often driven by rival dominance-seekers rather than the greater good. This book shows how leaders in one specific time and place pushed past the paralysis and built something.

The book also provides an interesting perspective on our modern sense of safety. When the horse-drawn streetcars of Paris had double-deckers added, people fell off the top and died. Yet those streetcars were considered a great success. Today, this would be a scandal. Accusations would fly until we figured out who failed to anticipate the risk and implement preventative measures. Our world is indeed safer because of all this finger-pointing. Some risks are not anticipated and prevented, so we hear a lot of outrage. When prevention efforts work, we hardly notice. Some safety measures emerge precisely because an ambitious person mercilessly disparages their predecessors to advance their career. This is what mammals do, but we can appreciate the benefits that come with the frustrations.

IN SUMMARY

The life stories in this section demonstrate the profound impact of early experience. We don't always know the facts of a person's childhood, but when we do, it's so clearly the foundation of their later expectations. Here are some powerful examples.

Longitude's John Harrison was given a watch when he was bedridden with smallpox at age six. For weeks, he had nothing to do but take that watch apart and put it back together. That built brain circuits that stayed with him, and supported insights that other people didn't have. He also built brain circuits for carpentry in his youth while assisting his father. As soon as he was old enough to choose his own steps, he designed a clock made from wood. Then he heard about the 1714 Longitude Prize. He had good reason to expect that reward. Accidents of experience had already adapted his brain for just such a task.

Napoleon III's mother always told him he was destined to rule France. There was no good reason to expect this because he grew up in lonely exile in Germany, after the fall of Napoleon I, with no French connection. But he built his skills, rode a train to Paris, and took over. His early expectations were his guide.

Semmelweis worked in an obstetrics clinic because he had gotten rejected from every other course of study he applied to. Obstetrics was the least prestigious job in the medical profession of his day. Semmelweis had so many rejections in his early career that he did not trust the goodwill of his colleagues. It's easy to see how that would burden his later efforts to communicate with them.

George VI was treated harshly in youth by his father, by the servants who raised him, and even his schoolmates. His brain learned to expect rebuke, and to surge with threat chemicals when he dared to speak.

The Sicilian Girl said nothing when she witnessed her father's murder at age eleven in order to save her life. She invested her do-something energy into a journal that recorded the comings and goings of the killers. Seven years later, when the Mafia went on to kill her brother, her extensive records helped the police convict them.

Mario Puzo grew up surrounded by mafiosi. Imagine a child watching his respected older brother become a "man of respect." Imagine a child worried about money seeing all that cash. His brain built circuits that were ready to be fleshed out with details later on.

Mary Leakey had extensive contact with archeologists at age eleven. She saw how they loved their work and how they got respect. More important, they respected Mary as a participant in their discussions with her parents. It's easy to see how her brain had wired itself to expect rewards from being an archeologist.

Mary Leakey's archeology brain circuits go even deeper. A century before she was born, one of her ancestors discovered stone-age artifacts in an English quarry. The distant cousin even found flint hand axes like those Mary spent her life digging up in Africa. The ancestor published an essay with the Society of Antiquaries, asserting the remoteness of human origins. His insights were too far ahead of their time and were not well received. Mary heard about this relative at an "impressionable" age, and she finished the work he started.

In *Wildlife Wars*, Richard Leakey says he was highly motivated to leave home and support himself from a young age. This meshes with Mary Leakey's comment that her husband was especially harsh with Richard, as if they were competitors. This is how it works in a gorilla family. When a young male reaches puberty, his father starts treating him as an opponent and the young gorilla leaves for his own safety. When young Richard set out on his own, he had no intention of going into his father's business. But he had spent his early years carrying dirt at dig sites and learning the methodology that goes with being a scientist. He had wired himself with high-level skills without knowing it, and eventually put those skills to good use.

Booker T. Washington had to work as a child, even after slavery had been outlawed in the United States. He longed to get an education, and waited years for the opportunity. That built his lifelong desire to help people get an education. Washington was thrilled when he got a chance to learn. Today's children in the United States are required to attend schools, and are not thrilled about learning all too often. Many take school for granted, or see it as pain to avoid. School feels rewarding compared to child labor, but when you compare it to games and modern distractions, the rewards are less immediately obvious. Today's expectation that learning should be fun sometimes gives students the power to reject learning if they say it's not fun. This is a vicious cycle because few things in life are fun until you've built basic circuits to process them. Children empowered to reject learning fail to build basic circuits for learning, and this damage is hard to undo. Booker T. Washington embraced learning because his early experience made it seem like "fun."

USE YOUR CIRCUITS

Each brain builds big circuits in its early years, and these circuits are so efficient that we rely on them throughout life. The point is not to blame your parents, but to know how your brain creates your world. You don't have to blame the world for your ups and downs when you know how you are creating them yourself.

Your early experience was unique. It wired you to see the world in a unique way. You can use your unique lens on the world to do something other people can't do. Instead of mourning the circuits you don't have, you can put the circuits you have to good use.

KEEP IN TOUCH

I hope you will follow the Inner Mammal Institute and post a review of this book online. I also hope you will write to me if you discover a new way to make peace with your inner mammal.

Contact me at InnerMammalInstitute.org where you will find plenty of resources to help you rewire your inner mammal.

INDEX

ABOUT THE AUTHOR

Loretta Graziano Breuning grew up surrounded by unhappiness and determined to make sense of it. She was not convinced by theories of human motivation she learned in school, so she kept searching. When she learned about the impact our brain chemicals have on animals, human frustrations suddenly made sense. So she retired from teaching and founded the Inner Mammal Institute.

Dr. Breuning is Professor Emerita of Management at California State University, East Bay. She holds a PhD from Tufts University, and a BS from Cornell University, both in multidisciplinary social science. Her other books include: *Habits of a Happy Brain: Retrain Your Brain to Boost Your Serotonin, Dopamine, Oxytocin, and Endorphin Levels*, and *I, Mammal: Why Your Brain Links Status and Happiness.* She writes the blog *Your Neurochemical Self* on PsychologyToday.com.

The Inner Mammal Institute provides tools that help people make peace with the animal inside. It has helped thousands of people learn to manage their neurochemical ups and downs. Discover your inner mammal at InnerMammalInstitute.org.

After college, Dr. Breuning spent a year in Africa as part of the United Nations Volunteers (UNV) program. She experienced the corruption pressures that undermine economic development, and determined to teach her students an alternative. She wrote the book *Grease-le$$: How to Thrive Without Bribes in Developing Countries,* and has lectured on that subject in China, Armenia, the Philippines, and Albania.

Today, she volunteers as a Docent at the Oakland Zoo, where she gives tours on mammalian social behavior. And she marvels each day at the overlap between a wildlife documentary and the lyrics to popular love songs.